BRITISH WRITERS AND THEIR WORK: NO. 9

General Editors

Bonamy Dobrée and T. O. Beachcroft

Editor of the American Edition

J. W. Robinson

BENJAMIN DISRAELI

by Paul Bloomfield

WILLIAM MAKEPEACE THACKERAY

by Laurence Brander

CHARLES DICKENS

by K. J. Fielding

ANTHONY TROLLOPE

by Hugh Sykes Davies

British writers and Their work

UNIVERSITY OF NEBRASKA PRESS · LINCOLN

Disraeli by Paul Bloomfield, *Thackeray* by Laurence Brander, *Trollope* by Hugh Sykes Davies (under the editorship of Bonamy Dobrée), and *Charles Dickens* by K. J. Fielding (under the editorship of T. O. Beachcroft) originally appeared separately in pamphlet form, published by Longmans, Green & Co. for The British Council and the National Book League [of Great Britain]. The Bison Book edition is published by arrangement with The British Council.

Manufactured in the United States of America

PREFACE

BRITISH WRITERS AND THEIR WORK is addressed to the student who wants a general introduction to a particular writer or group of writers, and also to the more advanced student and to the lover of literature who enjoys fresh, thoughtful literary criticism. Each volume includes essays on from two to six writers, the series as a whole being planned to consider British men of letters from the fourteenth century to the present day. The essays in most instances combine the biography of a writer with a critical appreciation of his work. Many of the contributors are themselves well-known English authors and critics.

The essays originally were published separately for The British Council under the titles listed on the copyright page. They are reprinted in the American edition with minor corrections.

It is hoped that not only will the essays prove useful and stimulating, but that the select bibliographies will make each volume a convenient, portable reference work. While the arrangement will vary somewhat from volume to volume, each essay usually is followed by a full list of the first editions of the writer's works (provided as a complement to the account in the essay); a list of collected editions, modern reprints, and student editions; a list of bibliographies and reference works; and a list of critical and biographical studies (including both standard works and other works found especially useful by the author of the essay). Each volume ordinarily concludes with a list of general works. The select bibliographies are based largely on the bibliographies originally published with the essays.

J. W. R.

CONTENTS

BENJAMIN DISRAELI

by Paul Bloomfield

BENJAMIN DISRAELI

From an engraving by an unknown artist reproduced in Monypenny
and Buckle's *Life. Reproduced here by permission of the
trustees of the British Museum.*

BENJAMIN DISRAELI was born on December 21, 1804, in London. He died in London on April 19, 1881, and is buried at Hughenden, Buckinghamshire.

DISRAELI

I

'**D**ISRAELI, Benjamin; Earl of Beaconsfield (1804–1881), statesman and man of letters.' This is how the Dictionary of National Biography introduces him. 'Without a study of his books,' wrote Monypenny, 'it is impossible to understand his life'. Ought we to understand his life? He was Prime Minister of Britain at the high tide of her nineteenth century power and influence, a dominating figure in British politics for a generation. That he, with his handicap of 'race', social obscurity and modest means, should have attained such a position already constitutes a claim to attention. For he was, as Lytton Strachey said—and Strachey weighed his words—'formidable—one of the most formidable men who ever lived'.

Formidable as a man and a statesman, but what concerns us here is the question whether, besides being formidable, he is, as a novelist, *readable*. He is readable, partly for the reason given by G. W. E. Russell, of the great Whig family opposed to Disraeli and his Tories. According to Russell, 'by far the acutest observer of our national life in the nineteenth century was Lord Beaconsfield, who combined the shrewdness of his race with unique opportunities of observation'. What was really unique about those opportunities was that he had to make them himself. And, even more remarkable, he announced his ambitions in his early novels while in process of achieving them. We can transpose Monypenny and say: 'Without a study of his life it is impossible to understand his books'—though not impossible to be highly entertained by them.

Disraeli was the second child and eldest son—he had a sister and two younger brothers—of a well-to-do Jewish man of letters, Isaac D'Israeli (this was how he spelt his name), of a Sephardi family settled in England since 1748.

An amiable, agnostic creature, who ceased to be a practising Jew without becoming a Christian, Isaac took a Gentile friend's advice and in 1817 arranged for his children to be received into the Church of England. Benjamin, as we shall see, became a Christian without for a moment feeling he had ceased to be a Jew. At least now he was not disqualified from public office, supposing he ever aspired to any such thing.

He was fond of his mother, fonder of his father, fondest of his affectionate and intelligent sister Sarah, the first of the women who, as he constantly insisted, played such a benign part in his life. His home background may therefore be said to have been an unusually congenial one. The schools he attended were quite good, without being fashionable. He never went to a university, instead he put in a year's hard reading by himself, an effort to which he alludes in *Vivian Grey* and *Contarini Fleming*, for in them, as in most of his novels, he is recollecting his own life-story when he is not anticipating it. In 1821 he was articled to a solicitor, but three years later he abandoned the law. He had begun to write; and so, of course, had scores of his contemporaries.

Thus in 1824, at the age of twenty, Disraeli, a converted Jew of middle-class family, with no influential connections, no great school behind him, no university degree, might have seemed one of the last young men likely to attain the highest office in the land. And in fact when he became Prime Minister for the first time in 1868 he was breaking some records. Never so far had there been a Cabinet Minister, let alone a Prime Minister, who was not of aristocratic family, or very wealthy, or educated at one of the great schools such as Eton, Westminster or Harrow, or who had not had two or all three of those advantages. Neither had there ever been (nor has there been since) a Prime Minister who had begun and ended his career by writing novels.

This much, then, is certain: the young Disraeli could take nothing for granted. Lacking all hereditary requisites for success in public life—except, as he would have said, one very significant one, namely his Jewish antecedents—he was going to have to think out his aims and his principles for himself. Luckily he did much of the thinking aloud, so to speak; he gave it expression in his books. The gift which enabled him to do so was not his only one. If the good fairies had not seen fit to direct him into what he would have called a 'patrician' cradle, their wands of enchantment assured him of courage, imagination, brains, and charm. Even before starting his self-questionings—what was he to aim at in life?—and his probings into the nature and functions of the political parties and the churches, he had taken his stand on two convictions from which he never budged. They were faith in what he rather misleadingly called 'race', and an absolute assurance that he, Benjamin Disraeli, was cut out for great things. By race he meant good breeding, but by Jewish race (which is not a true category) he meant something more esoteric. 'We belong to a race', he said in his old age to a Jewish boy, 'which knows how to do everything except to fail.' As for the importance of personality, he once said: 'It is the fashion of the present age to underrate the influence of individual character. For myself, I have ever rejected this consolation of mediocrity. I believe that everything that is great has been accomplished by great men.'

II

The ball opened in 1826 with the appearance of *Vivian Grey*. This novel of fashionable life and political machinations caused a stir because the publisher, Colburn, had hinted that its anonymous author had put many prominent persons into it under thin disguises. *Vivian Grey* is by no means a precocious *masterpiece*, like Dickens' *Pickwick*, and yet it has *precocity*—that is to say, a youthful verve and forwardness and boldness of imagination. In fact Disraeli knew hardly any prominent persons except his father's literary friends and the friends of the second of the women in his life, the vivacious Mrs Austen, a solicitor's wife, who had herself made a fair copy of the book and persuaded Colburn to publish it. However, it was not long before he found his way into the intellectual demi-monde, where the two reigning hostesses were those brilliant and much-wronged women Mrs Norton and Lady Blessington. When in due course he graduated into the Grand Monde of Society, he did not neglect them; he remained their affectionate champion and devotee. If his relationship with Mrs Austen became strained, it was because her husband, at first a generous patron, lost faith in him and made difficulties (as one can understand without altogether sympathising) over a loan of money.

A huge and bubbling book with an engaging brashness, *Vivian Grey* has several points of interest. In it Disraeli gives his readers a kind of prospectus of his intentions. An ambitious young man, Vivian Grey, finds a patron in the Marquess of Carabas, for whom he organises a party— including, comically enough, a Lord Beaconsfield, 'a very worthy gentleman, but between ourselves a damned fool'. In the 'eighteen-twenties generous-minded young men with a social conscience were dissatisfied with both the Tory and the Whig leadership, and were either Radicals or bent on reforming the existing parties. Reforming the Tory party became one of Disraeli's self-imposed tasks; meanwhile here is Vivian Grey throwing himself into the battle. Lord Carabas reads from the *Morning Post*:

'We are informed that some alteration in the composition of the present administration is in contemplation; Lord Past Century, it is said, will retire; Mr Liberal Principles will have the ———; and Mr Charlatan Gas the ——— . . .'

It would have been impossible for a hawk to watch its quarry with eyes of a more fixed and anxious earnestness than did Vivian Grey the Marquess of Carabas as his Lordship's eyes wandered over the paragraph.

No indeed!—for politics was Vivian Grey's ruling passion, as it was to become his creator's. 'I wish to act what I write', Disraeli confessed some years later. 'My works are the embodiment of my feelings. In *Vivian Grey* I have portrayed my real ambition.' But in it he portrayed some of his other predispositions as well. An off-hand Byronic cynicism about the socially Great combined with a taste for High Life and for the good things of life, including good food. Respect for the learned and the wise, as here represented by Vivian's father, a portrait of his own father. Deference to the rôle played by women in affairs of state by their hold on the male *dramatis personae*.

Disraeli's imagination was always haunted, his books show, by certain archetypal figures. There was an Apollonian youth, with a touch of Mercury, who as time went on softened, it may seem incongruously, into a kind of Candide. With his own increase in self-confidence and power, Vivian Grey, Contarini Fleming and Coningsby gave way to Tancred, Lothair and Endymion (all six the eponymous heroes of as many novels). Since this metamorphosis was correlated with his own transformation from an obscure young man into a Prime Minister, the psychological analysis is easy. In his own words, 'Everybody has a right to be conceited until he is successful'.

If the archetypal hero gradually became toned down, it was the other way round with the Mentor or Sage, for the progress from Mr Grey to the Sidonia of later novels was steeply upwards. Luckily for Disraeli's readers, his archetypal Woman bears not the remotest resemblance to the insipid or arch maidens who infest English nineteenth century fiction. She is strong: a young Diotima or prophetess, an Egeria. Exceptionally, in *Vivian Grey* the leading woman is a *bad* woman.

When it came out, as of course it soon did, that the author of *Vivian Grey* was nobody in particular, and that it was a waste of time to look for the real identities of his characters (except in one or two obvious instances— thus Lord Past Century was the Chancellor Eldon and the Duke of Waterloo the Duke of Wellington), a storm broke over Disraeli's head. This afflicted him sufficiently for him to make a similar bother give a turn for the worse to the fortunes of his hero in *Contarini Fleming*, published six years later. Perhaps the apparent set-back had something to do with his bad health in 1827; and yet by the spring of the following year he had the resilience to produce his amusing satire, *The Voyage of Captain Popanilla*.

It is not enough to say of this little book, which is stylised in the Voltairean manner, that it ridicules the Utilitarians, since it also sheds light on the author's intellectual evolution. He was one of the first in the field against those well-meaning (and indeed effective) theorists. The loud personalist booming of Carlyle had not yet been heard, and *Oliver Twist* was still to come. In any case Dickens, for all his incomparable genius, was such a child when it came to social theory and administration that G. M. Young was justified in calling his political satire 'tedious and ignorant'. Carlyle, it is true, like Disraeli, believed in immaterial values, personality, and the need for strong leadership, but even his best friends recognised he could not be trusted with the management of so much as a magazine. Disraeli, on the other hand, was born to manage the affairs of a nation and an empire.

Popanilla, native of Fantaisie, a Utopian island in the Indian Ocean, finds a box packed with Benthamite literature washed up on the beach. He reads it, is converted, and at once sets out to proselytize his king and fellow-countrymen. He explains to them:

> that man was not born for himself but for society; that the interests of the body are alone to be considered, and not those of the individual; and that a nation might be extremely happy, extremely powerful, and extremely rich, although every member of it might at the same time be miserable, dependent and in debt.

Though this is an echo of Pangloss's axiom in Voltaire's *Candide* that 'les malheurs particuliers font le bien general', times were ripe for the warning to be repeated. In more than one great nation at present the Utilitarian principles, stiffened by Marxism, have swept the board. In Victorian England the compromise worked out between Liberal laissez-faire and Disraelian humanist Toryism allowed the individual, and allows him to this day, to preserve his freedom of thought and contract and his idiosyncrasies ... How the king and people of Fantaisie rid themselves of Popanilla by sending him on an embassy to Hubbabub (London), capital of Vraibleusia, that is Trueblueland or England, and the account of what he saw and did there, all goes to make an amusing enough political essay, even if it creaks a little in places. The main point is that we find Disraeli coming out as an energetic defender of those personal values which, he realized, were being threatened, as much by the new industrial civilization as by the Benthamite philosophy.

Popanilla was fun, but it buttered no beans, and the author, partly owing to some rash speculations, was in debt; he badly needed money. He therefore wrote a second novel of fashionable life, *The Young Duke* (1831). His father was puzzled. 'What does Ben know of Dukes?' What Ben knew was that there was a public for descriptions of High Life, just as there is one today for paragraphs about the private affairs and goings-on of film stars. And although he afterwards said 'until my return from the East on the eve of the 1832 election I had lived a very secluded life and mixed not at all with the world', he was already acquainted with some of the most brilliant young men of family of his own generation. The famous little dinner he attended at Bulwer Lytton's house, alluded to nearly fifty years later in *Endymion*, took place while he was writing *The Young Duke*. Present also were Henry Bulwer, Lord Clarendon's nephew Charles Villiers, and Alexander Cockburn, a future Lord Chief Justice of England, and Henry Bulwer afterwards recorded that, 'if on leaving the table we ... had been asked which was the cleverest of the party we should have been obliged to say "the man in the green velvet trousers" '.

Disraeli only over-dressed *as if* he was decadent, but his young duke in the novel is presented as truly decadent and spoilt—'Let me die eating ortolans to the sound of soft music' is the least noxious kind of sentiment we get from him before his reform. If Disraeli was not yet perfectly documented about the gilded life, he could always invent—and so he freely did, as novelists do. The Duke of St. James, like most of Disraeli's heroes, was destined to be redeemed—whether from *Weltschmerz* or political heresy or, as in this case, his bad habits—by a good woman. Now our heroine this time was a Roman Catholic girl, Mary Dacre, which was significant not only because it reflected the author's approval of Catholic Emancipation, but because he, a tolerant Christianized Jew, was coming more and more to feel that, since man is a religious being, the Churches had as much an imperative duty to help preserve culture as they formerly had a pre-eminent part in creating it.

Another regular Disraelian feature of the book is the introduction of living personalities, here given ultra-topicality by a brisk and trenchant commentary on parliamentary debate. ('I hear that Mr Babington Macaulay is to be returned. If he speak half as well as he writes the House will be in fashion again.') Among the author's asides there is one that Monypenny calls 'a truly astonishing bit of prescient impertinence'.

> One thing is quite clear,—that a man may speak very well in the House of Commons and fail very completely in the House of Lords. There are two distinct styles requisite: I intend in the course of my career, if I have time, to give a specimen of both. In the Lower House, *Don Juan* may perhaps be our model; in the Upper House, *Paradise Lost*.

And so, while nobody has ever suggested that this lively book is one of Disraeli's masterpieces, there is nothing of *feuilleton* flatulence about it. On the £500 his publisher

advanced him, Disraeli set out accompanied by his sister's
fiancé, William Meredith, on a tour of the Mediterranean
and the Middle East.

III

The pair visited Spain, Malta, Corfu, Albania, Greece,
Cyprus, Turkey, Palestine, and Egypt. Disraeli, to judge
by his own and other people's accounts, seemed to be
impersonating one of the more colourful heroes of his early
novels. The exoticism of his clothes made people wonder
whether this Englishman was wearing fancy dress, and his
deliberately mannered behaviour did not always go down
quite as well with other Englishmen as he thought it was
doing. Soon after the two travellers had been joined at
Malta by their friend James Clay with his servant, Disraeli
in one of his many lively letters to his family wrote:

> To govern men, you must either excel them in their accomplish-
> ments, or despise them. Clay does one; I do the other ... Yesterday
> in the racket court, sitting in the gallery among strangers, the ball
> entered, and lightly struck me, and fell at my feet. I picked it up,
> and observing a young rifleman excessively stiff, I humbly requested
> him to forward its passage into the court, as I really had never
> thrown a ball in my life.

Clay's servant, by the way, was Giovanni Battista Falcieri,
known to fame as Tita: 'Byron died in his arms, and his
moustachios touch the earth.' At the end of the tour Disraeli
took Tita over, kept him employed and content till his
death more than forty years later, and then had no difficulty
in persuading Queen Victoria to pension his widow.

By the time Disraeli had spent a week in Jerusalem, it
would be less true to say that the East was casting its spell
on him than that he found there something he was more or
less consciously looking for, a sense of mystic communion
with the genius of his ancestors. Characteristically, he was

not satisfied to store up his impressions, but replanned a book he had had in mind for some years, *Alroy*, conceived a second, *Contarini Fleming*, and set to work on both of them; as if this was not enough he also made up his mind to stand for Parliament at the first opportunity—there were to be two strings to his bow. He returned to England, in October 1831, in excellent health but distress of spirits; Meredith had died of cholera in Cairo. Sarah Disraeli lived out her life unmarried, devoting herself to her brother.

Contarini Fleming: A Psychological Romance (1832) is an Aladdin's cave of so much strangely assorted treasure, that one can equally understand why the poet Heine praised it for its 'Gothic richness' and why it is less often reprinted than the tidier and more topical *Sybil* or *Lothair*. These are no doubt also in a sense better books, though Disraeli himself did not think so: he regarded *Contarini* 'as the perfection of English prose and a chef d'oeuvre'. (His boasting usually had something of Oscar Wilde's flippancy —as when he said to a lady who asked him if he had read such-and-such a novel: 'Madam, when I want to read a good novel I write one.') *Contarini* is no exception to the rule by which the creatures of Disraeli's imagination move on the highest social levels, preferably close to the throne, where there is one. (In *Endymion* the hero's sister is actually promoted to one of those exalted seats.) Young Fleming, with his noble Saxon father and noble Venetian mother— reflecting respectively Disraeli's ideas about his own nurture and nature—oscillates more violently between Art and Action than the author himself ever did. The object of the sort of action he himself had in mind was to get power, and power, as he already knew both from what he had observed of the world and from introspection, was liable to corrupt. He has the frankness to correlate Contarini's rise in the political world with a progressive, though not permanent, deterioration of character; I realize, he seems to say, that this is what can easily happen to an ambitious, able young man. But at the height of his success Contarini has misgivings.

Alone at a window, watching the sun set over a distant horizon: 'I felt indeed a disgust for all the worldliness on which I had been late pondering. And there arose in my mind a desire to create things beautiful as that golden sun and that glittering star.'

The publication of an indiscreet book, *Manstein*—Contarini's *Vivian Grey* so to speak—precipitates him into the course for which he, unlike Disraeli, had the greater temperamental inclination. He opts for art—in spite of his father's prophecy: 'My son, you will be Prime Minister . . .' in spite of much advice from the usual Sage, this time an artist called Winter, who oddly enough counsels action: 'Act without ceasing, and you will no longer talk of the vanity of life.' There is no doubt that Good Advice—both offering it and seeking it—is an ancient and perennial Jewish addiction, though when it comes to *taking* it there is little to distinguish Jew from Gentile. It is as if the People of the Book had Prophecy and Proverbs in their blood. Though at times, especially when Sidonia is being oracular in the later novels, we may become restive, Disraeli's sense of humour is seldom eclipsed for long at a time. 'Talk to women', Baron Fleming advises his son, 'talk to women as much as you can. This is the best school. This is the way to gain fluency, because you need not care what you say, and had better not be sensible.'

Greater works than *Contarini Fleming* have been patchy, scarred rather than marred by melodrama, bathos or irrelevances, but with something of all three of these flaws it is an interesting variation on the theme that character is fate—'destiny is our will', Contarini proclaims, 'and our will is our nature'. It is a revealing book, as it was meant to be, though it is strange that Disraeli should have bracketed *Alroy*, which came out in the following year, with *Vivian Grey* and *Contarini Fleming*, saying 'this trilogy is the secret history of my feelings—I shall write no more about myself'. He was better than his word and went on writing about himself to within a few days of his death. We must believe he was sincere when he said at the time that *Alroy* was his 'ideal ambition', but if ever he dreamt of starting or leading a Zionist movement it was not for long. The whole trend of his thinking was in quite another direction. It might have been otherwise today. As it was, he did the Jews everywhere a good turn by becoming one of the most admired men in Britain.

Alroy, a romanticised history of a twelfth-century Jewish impostor under the Seljuks, whom Disraeli turned into a second Judas Maccabaeus and martyr for his faith, must not be under-rated, though it is over-rhetorical and a dead end, for Disraeli soon came round to the view that Judaism was fermenting Christianity and Christianity was leavened Judaism. There is more to interest us in the two *jeux d'esprit* he produced at about the same time, intellectual whimsies in the manner of the Greek satirist Lucian, *Ixion in Heaven* and *The Infernal Marriage*. In these two short, lively, irreverent pieces, he served notice that although he aspired to the highest rank and dignities he was not taking the socially Great at the valuation they liked those outside their charmed circle to put on them. Young Ixion, having been admitted to heaven by Jupiter, throws his weight about with Disraelian aplomb. Invited to write something in Minerva's album, he makes this contribution:

> I have seen the world, and more than the world; I have studied the heart of man, and now I consort with Immortals. The fruit of my tree of knowledge is plucked, and it is this, ADVENTURES ARE TO THE ADVENTUROUS.
>
> Written in the Album of Minerva, by
> IXION IN HEAVEN

'Adventures are to the adventurous'; these words might have been Disraeli's motto. He had already used them in *Alroy*, and Sidonia was going to repeat them, with as much gravity as if the sentiment had been quite original, in *Tancred*.

The Infernal Marriage is the marriage between Pluto and Proserpine, made, like the Ixion story, an occasion for much brilliant pastiche and nonsense, in a form that no-one but a born literary artificer would have dreamt of choosing. There are more allusions to current politics than in *Ixion*, more recognizable caricatures of well-known people, and the Titans are the Tories, the Olympians the Whigs. The juxtaposition of classic formulas with colloquialisms is sometimes very funny. Earlier than this (and he was still only thirty) Disraeli had been pouring out, and all his life continued to pour out, aphorisms, not all of equal neatness, but some that deserve a place in the anthologies—like this one from Tiresias (the Duke of Wellington) in *The Infernal Marriage:* 'Next to knowing when to seize an opportunity, the most important thing in life is to know when to forego an advantage.' And when a young Titan, Rhoetus—who but Disraeli himself?—says to one of his companions 'that for his part he was convinced that the only way to beat the Olympians was to turn them to ridicule', we, wise after the event, perceive that a draught from the upper air had eddied down into the Realm of Twilight.

It was going to take more than ridicule to beat the Olympians—to unseat the Whigs. In 1830, while Disraeli was on his travels, they had come into power after an interminably long Tory innings. In 1832, the year of their great Reform Act, when Disraeli first tried and failed to enter Parliament, he met a Mr Wyndham Lewis, Member for Maidstone, with his wife, 'a pretty little woman', he wrote to his sister 'a flirt and a rattle'. It could not have entered his head that Mary Anne, married and twelve years older than himself, was one day going to become his wife and live with him for nearly thirty-five years—and in a state of model domesticity that was to be almost the only thing about him that his future rival, Gladstone, ever approved of. For the moment Disraeli was sceptical about love-marriages, and indeed not thinking of marriage for himself at all. 'All my friends who have married for love or beauty', he noted, 'either beat their wives or live apart from them. I may commit many follies, but I never intend to marry for love, which I am sure is a guarantee of infelicity.'

Politics were absorbing him more and more. Meeting Lord Melbourne at Mrs Norton's in 1834, he solemnly informed him: 'I want to be Prime Minister.' Even if the worldly Melbourne had not been impressed, he was too much a gentleman to laugh this off. But he shook his head. 'Nobody can compete with Stanley', he said, 'Stanley will be the next Prime Minister, you will see.' Melbourne lived long enough to be moved, by what he saw of Disraeli's progress, to exclaim: 'By God!—I believe the fellow will do it yet!'

Disraeli's political journalism of the year 1835 is consistent with those parts of his later novels in which he gave imaginative expression to his social ideals; he was to become, after all, the creator of 'the political novel', and with him life, journalism, politics, literature, were all of a piece—his story is singularly free from digressions. In the *Letters of Runnymede*, contributed to *The Times*, and in a book, *Vindication of the English Constitution*, which he dedicated to his powerful new friend, the American-born Lord Chancellor Lyndhurst, he is less convincing in his damning of the Whigs than when defending the old, or recommending the new, Toryism, that is to say, his own brand of it.

For 'beating the Olympians', Rhoetus in his own person was inclined to use strong language rather than ridicule. Even if there was something in his charge that the great Whig families had crystallized into 'a Venetian Oligarchy', it had been in process, first, of establishing the Hanoverian kings firmly on that throne for the mystique of which Disraeli had so much piety, and secondly, of saving England from revolution by bowing to the demand for political reform. More lately they had identified themselves with Disraeli's *bêtes noires*, the Utilitarians, because they realized that without what we should describe as bureaucratic measures there was no hope of dealing with a situation of unprecedented complexity. England was the first country to experience an industrial revolution, her death-rate was down and her birth-rate up, and nearly everywhere people were on the move pell-mell from the rural districts to the new towns. There was, however, some substance in Disraeli's fears that if bureaucracy got out of hand it would take the geniality out of people's dealings with one another. Everybody could see that society was being transformed: let it not be into a soulless mechanism. 'He demanded', as V. S. Pritchett has well said, 'the glory of a dogma, the sensation of re-birth, the emotion of a new era.' Dogma and the concept of re-birth are associated with religion. Sure enough in the *Vindication*, as in his later novels, he insisted that it was the duty of the clergy to resist materialism with more spirit than they seemed to be doing.

Meanwhile—he had fallen in love. His liaison with the emotional Lady Sykes seems to have begun in 1834 and lasted till August 1836, when he wrote in his diary: 'Parted for ever from Henrietta.' If *marrying* for love was 'a guarantee of infelicity', an affair of that kind continued too long might be fatal equally to happiness and wordly prospects. All the more so as his mistress, though affectionate, was neither stable nor adequately provided for by her complaisant husband, the father of her four children. Disraeli broke with her when he found she had been unfaithful to him, and sublimated the pain of parting in a novel, *Henrietta Temple: a Love Story*.

In this book, and in his next one, *Venetia*, he was dealing, as he himself put it, with 'feelings more enduring than public passions'. But this is not to say that *Henrietta Temple* is memorable for its love-interest alone, feelingly though this is developed. Every day of his life Disraeli's circle of acquaintance among influential people had been widening, so that by now his father would have acknowledged that he even knew something about dukes; and his travels had given him an insight into the manners and customs of the official British overseas. For the new novel he drew freely on his enlarged experience. The hero, Ferdinand Armine, is at Malta with his regiment; he is poor but of course of 'good' family, and—once more 'of course'—in need of a good woman to redeem him from his bad habits (preferably too from his penury). Since he makes up to the first good woman who comes his way, his cousin Katherine, because she is an heiress and not because he loves her, he seems to be going—from a moral point of view—from bad to worse. Then Henrietta comes on the scene, and Ferdinand and she really fall in love. The skein of the plot is disentangled by the diplomacy of the benevolent Count Alcibiades de Mirabel, a portrait—too flattering to be a true likeness—of Disraeli's friend Count d'Orsay. Among other recognizable characters is Lady Bellair, in life the eccentric old hostess and lion-hunter Lady Cork, to whom in her girlhood Dr. Johnson had said 'dearest, you're a dunce', and who, when approaching her ninetieth birthday had called *The Infernal Marriage* 'the finest book ever written'.

If what Disraeli's public there and then got, besides an impassioned love-story, was something of a *roman a clé*, what posterity gets is the love-story as before and some social history. Though his first full-bodied *political* novel, *Coningsby*, was still to come, a small infusion of the essence of his political philosophy had been perceptible in *Vivian Grey*, and the doses were being gradually increased. Curiously enough, where English literature is concerned, Disraeli is the most outstanding apologist of the principle of *Noblesse Oblige*. He made it abundantly clear from the start that he already suspected how much extravagance, insensibility, jobbery, *chi-chi* and scandal there was in the highest circles, but he believed, and he continued all his life to believe—and he found ample evidence to support him—that the British ruling class in every generation threw up men prepared to rule, and to do so disinterestedly and capably, and without regard to their comfort, health, or domestic enjoyments. He was not deceived by titles ('dukes can be made!' he once exclaimed angrily when a duke kept him waiting) but expected to find good breeding among the well-bred. And, with the enlightened prejudice of a eugenist, he put Nature before Nurture—thus in *Contarini Fleming* he had made Winter say: 'nature is more powerful than education.' It never surprised him to find natural ability in a poor Jew or an underpaid mill-hand. If in *Henrietta Temple* the human decencies, together with charm and sagacity, are conspicuously embodied in Lord Montfort, heir to a dukedom, it is because this is relevant to the story he wanted to tell, as well as compatible with his romantic feeling for the English aristocracy.

Then about a year later, in May 1837, six months before the beginning of his great parliamentary career, he published *Venetia: or the Poet's Daughter*. This is the least self-regarding of his early novels, even if there is some identification of himself both with "Lord Cadurcis" and "Marmion Herbert", who stand respectively for Byron and Shelley. Writing under the shadow of debt, bad health and doubts about his chances of a political future, he threw himself imaginatively into the strange drama of the lives of the two poets. Byron's child Allegra becomes Marmion Herbert's Venetia, and Disraeli gives us one of our earliest sympathetic studies of a child growing up in a broken home. To the fictionalised presentation of Byron's career he brings not only his verve but delicacy and tact. And there is something else. English society had soon forgiven Byron for breaking certain rules (it is better to speak of rules than conventions, for the Great World was not very conventional) but Shelley, more neurotic, more of what today we should call an ideologist, was still under a cloud—though some of the Cambridge 'Apostles' had opened his defence. Is it strange that on the eve of important developments in his own mundane career the 'formidable' Disraeli too should have concerned himself with the poet's rehabilitation? By no means, for Shelley had been a prophet, and it was in a prophetic or messianic rôle that Disraeli saw himself.

IV

For eleven years he had been writing hard. The next seven made the first long break in his output. When the young Queen Victoria's first Parliament met in November 1837 he took his seat as one of the Tory Members for Maidstone. He owed his election to his fellow Member, Wyndham Lewis. On December 7 he made his maiden speech, an apparent failure, ending it with the famous words 'I sit down now, but the time will come when you will hear me.' In March 1838 Wyndham Lewis died, and the following year Disraeli married his widow, a woman of forty-six with an income of £4,000 a year. It is enough to say that posterity has been for ever disarmed by her own summing up of the affair long after: 'Dizzy married me for my money, but if he had the chance again he would marry me for love.'

So quickly after this did Disraeli make his political reputation that when in 1841 the Tories came in, under the eminent Sir Robert Peel, he stood an excellent chance of high office. Peel was ready to offer him an appointment, but young Lord Stanley objected. Stanley, of whom Melbourne and almost everyone else in politics still thought so highly, was arrogant and opinionated. He despised Disraeli, and told Peel that 'if that scoundrel were taken in [to the Ministry] he would not remain himself'. The ironies of what followed are remarkable. Peel soon lost both Stanley and Disraeli through his decision to repeal the duty on imported corn, and this forced Stanley to co-operate with Disraeli and, when in the process of time his health began to fail him, to hand over to 'that scoundrel' the reins of power.

Meanwhile, in the decade 1841–1851, there was Disraeli, first abandoned by his chief and then in opposition to him, and on bad terms with Stanley, the supposed hope of the orthodox Tories. The outlook had grown dark again. As usual, under such circumstances, Disraeli sat down and began to write, only this time there was a difference. It may be, as Monypenny says, that his exclusion from office in 1841 'led to . . . the creation of the political novel'. But though out of office the novelist was not out of politics. He was going one better than Contarini Fleming. For Disraeli it was to be both Art *and* Action.

Between 1841 and 1852, when he became Chancellor of the Exchequer for the first time under Stanley, Disraeli wrote four books, three of them novels that can more truly be called a trilogy than the earlier series of *Vivian Grey*, *Contarini Fleming* and *Alroy;* they were *Coningsby*, *Sybil* and *Tancred*. Then came a political biography, a life of Lord George Bentinck. We must attribute the temptation to think of *Coningsby* as the most Disraelian novel of them all to the enthusiasm the author put into it, and to the skill with which he here mixed all the ingredients at his disposal. The setting is contemporary social and political life; many well-known characters are introduced, some disguised and others under their own names; there is our first meeting with the most celebrated of the Disraelian Sages, Sidonia; and the whole is not only a commentary, often sparkling, but a forecast: *Coningsby; or the New Generation*, is the manifesto of 'Young England'. The future, as Disraeli meant it to be, is announced with topical emphasis, and the public had no difficulty in recognising his friends and followers in Coningsby himself (the Hon. George Smythe), Lord Henry Sydney (Lord John Manners) and Sir Charles Buckhurst (Alexander Cochran). It was a very small pressure group! But its members sat in Parliament, where they helped to make Disraeli's weight felt, if not their own.

What was it they stood for? We can infer a good deal of it from a sentence in *Coningsby* telling us what they disapproved of: 'a crown robbed of its prerogative, a Church extended to a Commission and an aristocracy that does not lead.' They believed it would be a mistake to abandon protection of home-grown corn, because this would mean a dangerous one-sided development of the nation's economy. Disraeli distinguished sharply between wealth and welfare, convinced there was now too much concentration on industry and making money. He and his disciples (in and out of *Coningsby*) wanted the country to be less of a machine, more of a living organism. Whatever a man's social status his individuality must be respected. When Coningsby first meets the great Sidonia he asks him a question:

> 'But what is an individual', Coningsby exclaimed, 'against a vast public opinion?' 'Divine', said the stranger. 'God made man in His own image, but the Public is made by Newspapers, Members of Parliament, Excise Officers, Poor Law Guardians.'

Reading the book, we are inducted into the mysteries of a ruling-class young man's political, social, and sentimental education in the England of the 1830s. And through what a wonderful portrait gallery of men and women in all walks of life our voluble, brilliant, well-informed guide conducts us! From the good and the beautiful to that mischievous old epicurean, Coningsby's grandfather, Lord Monmouth, his agent the time-serving Rigby, and the lesser wire-pulling types Mr Tadpole and Mr Taper, whose names have passed into English idiom. Monmouth, taken like Thackeray's Lord Steyne in *Vanity Fair* from the *bon vivant* Marquess of Hertford (who was dead), comes off better than Rigby, who was the politician Croker, an antagonist of Disraeli's (and still alive). Though Thackeray, in perhaps the most perfect of English novels, makes a memorable character of Lord Hertford, Disraeli's version plausibly suggests more of the kind of motives, besides lasciviousness, that would have explained his nature and behaviour.

The long-windedness of certain passages at the beginning and in the middle of *Coningsby* is due to the people in the story having too much to say, not to the author having too little. But when the plot gets under way it grips. Coningsby, a young man of high principles, is caught between his love for Edith, daughter of the estimable industrialist Millbank, and his duty to and indeed affection for his unscrupulous grandfather, Millbank's relentless enemy. In course of making everything end happily, Disraeli uses some shock tactics; on the other hand, he often proves that he knows very well that critical events are apt to be the result of what may seem trifles:

> There is no end to the influence of woman on our life. It is at the bottom of everything that happens to us. And so it was that, in spite of all the combinations of Lucretia [Monmouth's wife] and Mr. Rigby, and the mortification of Lord Monmouth, the favourable impression he casually made on a couple of French actresses occasioned Coningsby, before a month had elapsed since his memorable interview at Monmouth House, to receive an invitation again to dine with his grandfather.

No less severe a critic than Leslie Stephen said of *Coningsby* that 'it wants little but a greater absence of purpose to be a first-rate novel'. *Sybil; or The Two Nations*, which came out the following year (1845) and was dedicated to 'a perfect Wife', has even more purpose—and it is a finer book, still the most often read of Disraeli's works and perhaps the best thing he did. In *Coningsby* it is noticeable that, although Mr Millbank is a factory owner, the industrial background, the life of the factory workers, is hardly even sketched. If he had wanted to, Disraeli could have filled the picture in, as he now did in *Sybil*, for since his entry into Parliament he had been absorbed by social problems, and in the early 'forties—the 'Hungry Forties'—had paid visits to the industrial north to see conditions there with his own eyes. Already in 1839 he had puzzled both sides of the House of Commons by coming out in sympathy with the Chartists, those Radicals, mainly working-class, who were pressing for constitutional reform. In *Sybil* on the same occasion the aristocratic hero, Charles Egremont, makes a speech in the House very like Disraeli's own:

> 'It was a very remarkable speech of Egremont', said the grey-headed gentleman. 'I wonder what he wants.'

'I think he must be going to turn Radical', said the Warwickshire peer.

'Why, the whole speech was against Radicalism', said Mr. Egerton.

'Ah, then he is going to turn Whig, I suppose.'

'He is an ultra anti-Whig', said Egerton.

'Then what the deuce is he?' said Mr. Berners.

'Not a Conservative, certainly, for Lady St. Julians does nothing but abuse him.' . . .

'That speech of Egremont was the most really democratic speech that I ever read', said the grey-headed gentleman.

'Democratic' is a much-abused word, but nobody can read *Sybil* and not acknowledge that Disraeli's indignation at social injustice was passionately felt. The first novel of its kind, it presented the Rich with an authentic and devastating picture of the life led by the Poor—starving weavers, iron-workers sunk in squalor, harassed peasants breaking up the new-fangled machinery which they blamed for their misfortunes. Two years earlier in an essay, *Past and Present*, Thomas Carlyle had expressed something like Disraeli's opinions—a book that might have caused popular disturbances, Monckton Milnes thought, if Carlylye had written it in plain English and it had been widely read. Oddly enough Carlyle regarded Disraeli as 'an absurd monkey dancing on John Bull's chest'. He lived to see him as Prime Minister thirty years later, passing laws that might have been drawn up by Coningsby and Egremont—with some help from the author of *Past and Present*.

The Rich and the Poor, those were 'the Two Nations'. To mark the contrasts between them Disraeli opens *Sybil* at the Jockey Club in London, where 'in a golden saloon that . . . in its splendour would not have disgraced Versailles', the idler rich are placing bets for the Derby of 1837. Then he quickly translates us to a very different spot.

This town of Marney was a metropolis of agricultural labour, for the proprietors of the neighbourhood having for the last half-century acted on the system of destroying the cottages on their estates, in order to become exempted from the maintenance of the population, the expelled people had flocked to Marney, where, during the war, a manufacturer had afforded them some relief . . .

But the factory wheels had long stopped turning.

The local magnate is the callous Lord Marney; his brother Charles Egremont is another sort, and the hero of the book. Looking for deliverance from his perplexities, he meets Sybil, the daughter of a Roman Catholic mill-manager, and she confirms him in his popular sympathies. But he follows her neither into Catholicism nor Chartism. Disraeli, after all, was never a Jacobin, so for Egremont as for him the watchword once again is *noblesse oblige*. If this is not socialism, neither is it a plea for preserving class distinctions. In *Coningsby* we read of Sydney's ducal mother that she had 'that perfect good breeding which is the result of nature and not of education, for it may be found in a cottage and may be missed in a palace'. Disraeli, in fact, equates good breeding with good nature, and good nature with an upright character—the product of what, if not of good breeding? He never altogether admits that people are often the creatures of their conditions. Yet, from the propaganda he made in *Sybil* and from what he did when he became Prime Minister, we can see how important he knew it was to *improve* conditions.

The contrasts of *Sybil*, the warning conveyed in the vivid scenes of riot and violence (which England was to be spared in 1848, the Year of Revolutions), the threads of idealism running through the book, and much bracing dialogue, add up to something impressive, and the whole is, as a work of fiction should be, greater than the sum of the parts.

If it had not been for the political crisis of 1846 over the repeal of the Corn Laws, *Tancred* would have come out even harder on the heels of *Sybil* than it did. This last volume of the trilogy was published in 1847; after examining the political scene and the condition of the people, Disraeli had turned to the most fundamental problem of all, that of belief. 'I do not believe in belief', said E. M. Forster in 1939. This was honest of him, but Disraeli's exclamation seventy-five years earlier, 'man is a being born to believe', was on the mark. When in 1864 he told an Oxford audience 'I am on the side of the Angels', he was not setting up as a fundamentalist, but repeating that he believed in belief—believed, that is to say, that man, whatever his ancestry, is a spiritual being.

Tancred, or the New Crusade is a curious book, even for a book by Disraeli. English literature does not abound in heroes who are seeking for the Truth. Such a one however is Tancred, Lord Montacute, a young nobleman with every advantage in life, except that he does not know what to *believe*. He astonishes his sympathetic parents, the Duke and Duchess of Bellamont, by telling them he feels he ought to make a pilgrimage to the Holy Sepulchre, as a crusading forbear of his had done six centuries ago:

> 'I, too, would kneel at that tomb; I too, surrounded by the holy hills and sacred groves of Jerusalem, would relieve my spirit from the bale that bows it down; would lift my voice to heaven, and ask, What is DUTY, and what is FAITH? What ought I to DO, and what ought I to BELIEVE?

Lady Bellamont would not have minded his going to Holland—'a Protestant country, and there are no vermin'. But Jerusalem! A bishop is called in, to try to head the eccentric young man from his purpose. Is there no religious inspiration to be found in England? He says complacently to Tancred:

> 'We shall soon see a bishop at Manchester.'
> 'But I want to see an angel at Manchester.'
> 'An angel!'
> 'Why not? Why should there not be heavenly messengers when heavenly messages are most wanted?'

So the bishop having failed, the Bellamonts resort to a man of the world, Lord Eskdale. By luring Tancred into 'Society', where he meets the fetching Lady Constance, Eskdale almost succeeds. But although Lady Constance has 'guanoed her mind' by reading French novels and some modern science, she says too much. She presses on Tancred a book on evolution which explains 'everything':

> First there was nothing, then there was something; then, I forget the next, I think there were shells, then fishes; then we came; let me see; did we come next? Never mind; we came at last. And the next change there will be something very superior to us, something with wings. Ah! that's it: we were fishes, and I believe we shall be crows. But you must read it.

'I was a fish, and I shall be a crow . . . What a spiritual mistress!' Tancred says to himself—and gets ready for his pilgrimage. Disraeli's satire here shows him at once abreast with the times and allergic to some of the inferences that were going to be hastily made from Darwin's *Origin of Species* when it came out twelve years after *Tancred*. But on the eve of leaving England Tancred agrees to consult one more oracle, none other than Sidonia. 'It appears to me, Lord Montacute', this eminent Jewish banker says to him, 'that what you want is to penetrate the great Asian mystery.' If A. J. P. Taylor is right, and if 'Disraeli increased the obstacles in his path for the pleasure of overcoming them', then to introduce this theme of an 'Asian mystery' was for once a miscalculation, for he never heard the end of it in his life-time, and only the other day Dr. Taylor was declaring that the reason why he never revealed the mystery was because there was nothing to reveal.

But there is really no doubt what the mystery was, that Tancred set out to 'penetrate' in the second and longer part of the book. Disraeli believed in 'a divine reality substantial to the world of things and lives and minds' (Aldous Huxley's words), and it was this perennial philosophy that he hoped

to convey in *Tancred*. In one view his mistake was to over-
emphasise the rôle of the Jewish people, the Chosen People,
as the depositories of divine revelation, though it is hardly
for the stricter sort of Christians to find fault with this. On
aesthetic grounds, however, they might recoil from
Tancred's ardours and exaltations—and from the anti-
climax of the end: 'The Duke and Duchess of Bellamont
have arrived in Jerusalem.'

It happened that the year after *Tancred* was published
Sidonia's original, Baron Lionel de Rothschild, was elected
Member of Parliament for the City of London. He was not
allowed to sit because, as a Jew, he could not take his oath
'on the true faith of a Christian'. The City voters went
on obstinately re-electing him until the matter was at last
put right under the second Derby-Disraeli administration
in 1858. Disraeli had carried on the fight in the House of
Commons, where most Members were not very pleased
when he reminded them:

> All the early Christians were Jews. The Christian religion was first
> preached by men who had been Jews till they were converted;
> every man in the early ages of the Church by whose power, or
> zeal, or genius the Christian faith was propagated, was a Jew.

Then in chapter 24 of his Life of his dead friend, the
protectionist, Lord George Bentinck (1851), he faced about
and asked the Jews to consider it an honour that 'the
Queen of Heaven' should be a Jewess, and 'that the redemp-
tion of the human race has been effected by a child of Israel':
he was again preaching that Christianity is perfected
Judaism. But the children of Israel were no more edified
than the Members of Parliament had been.

V

After the life of Bentinck there was a break of nearly
twenty years in his literary production. The time for action

had come. In 1852 he was Chancellor of the Exchequer under Stanley, now Earl of Derby, and Queen Victoria told her uncle: 'Mr Disraeli (*alias* Dizzy) writes very curious reports to me ... much in the style of his books.' Twenty-five years later such reports had become one of her chief pleasures in life, and their author her intimate friend. Disraeli was in again with Derby in 1866; their Reform Bill of 1867 gave urban working class men the vote; in 1868 Derby retired and Disraeli was for the first time Prime Minister. 'By God!' Melbourne would have exclaimed if he had been alive, 'the fellow has done it!'

Some months later the Government fell. Cheerfully the Tory leader, who was now sixty-five, sat down and wrote a novel, *Lothair*, which appeared twenty-three years after *Tancred*. Lothair is yet another wealthy young nobleman wondering 'what I ought to DO, and what I ought to BELIEVE'. But we must let Disraeli have some credit for returning again to this serious theme, evidence of his deep and life-long moral earnestness; as subjects go this one will never stale.

Unlike Tancred, Lothair does not at first strike out on a line of his own, and indeed he is, or appears to be, so malleable that Leslie Stephen said he was 'unpleasantly like a fool'. But neither are the fools of life or fiction necessarily unpleasant, nor does it much matter if Lothair was susceptible. On the contrary, it would have been fatal if he had not been, since the plot and purpose of the book required him to respond to three young women representing three attitudes to duty and belief, and in the end to point Disraeli's moral by getting himself tied up with the right one. G. W. E. Russell thought *Lothair* Disraeli's masterpiece, and well he might, considering the skill and insight that went to creating the three heroines. These were the apostle of international revolution, the beautiful and passionately committed Theodora Campian; the charming and pious Roman Catholic, Clare Arundel; and Lady Corisande. When Lothair has nearly lost his life at Mentana, fighting

for Garibaldi against the successful French defenders of
Rome, it is Clare who nurses him back to health. But when
he sees the 'official' Papal account of what happened he is
startled. He expostulates with Cardinal Grandison.

> 'Good God!' exclaimed Lothair. 'Why! take the very first allegation,
> that I fell at Mentana fighting in the ranks of the Holy Father.
> Everyone knows that I fell fighting against him, and that I was
> almost slain by one of his chassepots. It is notorious . . .' . . .
> 'I know there are two narratives of your relations with the battle
> of Mentana,' observed the Cardinal quietly. 'The one accepted as
> authentic is that which appears in this journal; the other account,
> which can only be traced to yourself, bears no doubt a somewhat
> different character, but . . . it is in the highest degree improbable . . .'
> 'I think,' said Lothair, with a kindling eye and a burning cheek,
> 'that I am the best judge of what I did at Mentana.'
> 'Well, well,' said the Cardinal with dulcet calmness, 'you naturally
> think so, but you must remember you have been very ill, my dear
> young friend, and labouring under much excitement.'

Though Disraeli gives Lady Corisande the least striking
personality of the three young women, he has the art to
make it seem inevitable that she should be Lothair's fate.
She is in the disciplined English tradition, Anglican and
moderate—three very good things to be, according to his
mature opinion, in a dangerous world. Europe seemed to
have passed into an Age of Conspiracy. The agitations of
those rival dissentients, Mazzini and Garibaldi, were nothing
to what might be expected if Marx or *his* rival, the
Anarchist Bakunin, had their way. Together with all the
regular Disraelian features *Lothair* offers a disturbing picture
of movements whose unfolding pattern the author saw in
clearer focus than most people in England.

Gladstone had another four years in power. It was at
a Gladstone reception that Disraeli hit off their mutual
antipathy in a crack as tactful as it is witty. On one of the
Gladstone girls asking him to identify a foreign grandee
for her, he answered: 'That, my dear young lady, is the most

dangerous statesman in Europe—except, as your father would say, myself . . . or, as I should prefer to put it, your father.'

Then in 1874 came his great chance. Prime Minister for six fruitful years, he sponsored a good deal of domestic legislation of more permanent significance than his purchase of the Suez Canal shares with the help of 'Sidonia' Rothschild or his triumph at the Congress of Berlin, where Bismarck, much impressed, said: 'The old Jew—that's the man!' His laws benefitted sailors, shop assistants, the Trade Union movement as a whole, and, by a Public Health Act, the nation as a whole. In April 1880 he was out; he was seventy-six, afflicted with gout, bronchitis and asthma—and yet by August he had put the finishing touches to his last complete novel, *Endymion*. He dedicated it to the charming grandmother, Lady Bradford, with whom he was conducting a romantic and rather uninhibited flirtation. 'I owe everything to woman', he had once written to her. This was not correct, but, as Buckle says, 'of Endymion, the hero of his last novel, it is true'.

In the story Endymion, with the help of his sister, his wife and other devoted women, becomes Prime Minister at the age of forty—as Disraeli wished he could have done. As in his other political novels, the treatment of situations, the elucidation of ideas, have priority, while the dialogues between the secondary figures—taken from life by that shrewd observer—contribute an extraordinary vivaciousness besides offering what to readers then was a spice of gossip, and to readers now is living history. *Endymion* has more portraits than any of its predecessors.

More than fifty years had passed since Vivian Grey had made his bold bid for a wordly success that in the end had eluded him, perhaps because his wordly wisdom, like his creator's at the time, had left so much to be desired. *Endymion* on the other hand is pervaded by 'the experience of the statesman who had taken his full share in the direction of great affairs'. It is a more tolerant book than *Lothair* or the Young England trilogy, and less idealistic—except that Disraeli showed he had never lost his confidence in 'youth', as he had also proved when in power by going out of his way to help promising young men.

How does one sum him up as a writer? Saintsbury, who admired his novels, said nobody had ever quite known how to classify them; indeed, according to Lord David Cecil, 'for all their brilliance, they are not strictly speaking novels', and according to Leslie Stephen, 'he was not exactly a humourist, but something for which the rough nomenclature of critics has not yet provided a distinctive name'. Trollope detested the whole body of his work, and spoke of it as if it consisted entirely of stories about people whose way of life he disapproved of, ignoring the salient fact that, as V. S. Pritchett put it, 'the novels of Disraeli tell us everything'. Given his talents, temperament, and the circumstances of his career, he was in a better position to do so than any novelist before or since. It is by no means a reproach if he tells us more about some things (high society and politics) and less about others than we get from more introvert authors who had not kept such a varied company nor been so interested in the social mechanism. Trollope himself might have found writing his political novels a severer task if Disraeli had not blazed the trail for him.

Of Disraeli's poems, early and rather derivative work, there is perhaps no need to say much here; *The Revolutionary Epick* is indeterminate, and though *Alarcos*, dramatized, had a certain *succes d'estime* at the time, it is not a thriller we are likely to see revived.

Of his prose fiction one can pronounce, uncontroversially, that, like his career, it is unique.

VI

Once *Endymion* was out, the old statesman went to it again. He had written nine chapters of yet another novel when

the pen almost literally dropped from his hand. The unfinished book was to be about life and death, about a young
man like Mr Gladstone long ago, about the spirit of
Revolution that had come into the world. The cold January
of 1881 proved fatal to the Earl of Beaconsfield (as he had
become in 1876). 'I beg you will be very good and obey
the doctors', the Queen wrote to him; but his time was up
and, on April 19, he died. He comes to life again like no
other statesman when we open one of his books. When we
shut them it is with an encouraging (not, as it could be,
an alarming) sense of the truth of Alroy's affirmation:

By what Man has done we learn what Man can do, and gauge
the power and prospects of our race.

BENJAMIN DISRAELI

Select Bibliography

BIBLIOGRAPHY

SADLEIR, MICHAEL. *Excursions in Victorian Bibliography*. London: Chaundy and Cox, 1922.

Contains a bibliography of Disraeli.

Note. The Disraeli archives preserved at Hughenden Manor are in the process of being listed under the auspices of the National Trust, the owner of the property.

COLLECTED EDITIONS

Collected Edition of the Novels and Tales. 10 vols. London: Longmans, 1870–1871.

Novels and Tales. Hughenden edition. 11 vols. London: Longmans, 1881.

The Bradenham Edition of the Novels and Tales. With Introductions by P. Guedella. 12 vols. New York: Knopf, 1927.

The Novels. 11 vols. London: John Lane, 1927–1928.

SEPARATE WORKS

Dates of first London editions are given, and modern editions and current paperbacks are also recorded here.

NOVELS

Vivian Grey. 4 vols. 1826–1827.

The Voyage of Captain Popanilla, 1828.

The Young Duke. 3 vols. 1831.

Contarini Fleming: A Psychological Autobiography. 4 vols. 1832.

The Wondrous Tale of Alroy and the Rise of Iskander. 3 vols. 1833.

Henrietta Temple: A Love Story. 3 vols. 1837.

Venetia. 3 vols. 1837.

Coningsby: Or the New Generation. 3 vols. 1844.

Edited by L. N. Langdon-Davies (Everyman's Library); by André Maurois (The World's Classics); by Asa Briggs (Signet). For some interesting reactions to Coningsby, see *Anti-Coningsby: Or the Generation Grown Old* (1844), and *Strictures on Coningsby* (1844).

Sybil: Or the Two Nations. 3 vols. 1845.

Edited by W. Sichel (The World's Classics); Nelson Classics.

Tancred: Or the New Crusade. 3 vols. 1847.

Ixion in Heaven, the Infernal Marriage, Popanilla, Count Alarcos, 1853.

Lothair. 3 vols. 1870.

Nelson Classics.

Endymion. 3 vols. 1880.

Tales and Sketches. With a Prefatory Memoir by J. L. Robertson. 1891.

VERSE

The Revolutionary Epick. 2 vols. 1834; revised edition, 1864.

Edited with other poems, by W. Davenport Adams (London: Hurst, 1904).

The Tragedy of Count Alarcos, 1839.

The Dunciad of To-Day: A Satire, and the Modern Aesop. With an introduction by M. Sadleir. London: Ingpen and Grant, 1928.

POLITICAL WRITINGS

Lord George Bentinck: A Political Biography, 1852.

Edited by C. Whibley (London: Constable, 1905).

Whigs and Whiggism: Political Writings. Edited by W. Hutcheon. London: Murray, 1913.

Includes the following treatises (first published separately as dated): *What is He?* (1833); *The Crisis Examined* (1834); *Vindication of the English Constitution* (1835); *Letters of Runnymede* (1836); *The Spirit of Whiggism* (1836).

LETTERS

Home Letters, 1830–1852. Edited by A. Birrell. London: Cassell, 1928. Includes *Home Letters* (1830–1831), and *Disraeli's Correspondence with his Sister* (1886), both originally edited by R. Disraeli, and first reprinted together as *Lord Beaconsfield's Letters 1830–52* (1887).

Letters to Lady Chesterfield and Lady Bradford. Edited by Lord Zetland. 2 vols. New York: Appleton, 1929.

Letters to Frances Anne, Marchioness of Londonderry, 1837-61. Edited by the Marchioness of Londonderry. London: Macmillan, 1938.

SPEECHES

Church and Queen. Five Speeches, 1860-64, 1865.

Speeches on Parliamentary Reform, 1848-66. Edited by M. Corry. 1867.

Speeches on the Conservative Policy of the Last Thirty Years. Edited by J. F. Bulley. 1870.

Selected Speeches. Notes by T. E. Kebbel. 2 vols. London: Longmans, 1882.

The Radical Tory. Disraeli's Political Development. Illustrated from his Original Writings and Speeches. Edited by H. W. J. Edwards. London: Cape, 1937.

BIOGRAPHICAL AND CRITICAL STUDIES

MANNERS, J. (Duchess of Rutland). *Some Personal Recollections of the Earl of Beaconsfield.* Edinburgh: Blackwood, 1881.

O'CONNOR, T. P. *Lord Beaconsfield.* London: Mullan, 1879.

FROUDE, J. A. *Lord Beaconsfield.* New York: Harper, 1890. Everyman's Library, 1914.

LAKE, H. *Personal Reminiscences of Beaconsfield.* London: Cassell, 1891.

MEYNELL, W. *Disraeli. An Unconventional Biography.* New York: Appleton, 1903; revised edition, 1927.

SICHEL, WALTER. *Disraeli.* New York: Funk and Wagnalls, 1904.

MONYPENNY, W. F., AND BUCKLE, G. E. *The Life of Benjamin Disraeli, Earl of Beaconsfield.* 6 vols. New York: Macmillan, 1910-1920; revised edition, 2 vols. New York: Macmillan, 1929. The standard biography.

SOMERVELL, D. C. *Disraeli and Gladstone.* New York: Doran, 1926.

CLARKE, SIR EDWARD G. *Benjamin Disraeli 1804-81.* London: Murray, 1926.

MURRAY, DAVID L. *Disraeli.* London: Benn, 1927.

MAUROIS, ANDRÉ. *Disraeli.* Trans. H. Miles. New York: Appleton-Century, 1928.

THANE, E. *Young Mr. Disraeli.* New York: Harcourt, Brace, 1936.

STAPLEDON, R. G. *Disraeli and the New Age.* London: Faber and Faber, 1943.

POWELL, ANTHONY (ed.). *Novels of High Society from the Victorian Age*. London: Pilot, 1947.
Includes *Henrietta Temple*.

MASEFIELD, MURIEL. *Primroses and Peacocks. A Survey of Disraeli's Novels*. London: Bles, 1953.

JERMAN, B. R. *The Young Disraeli*. Princeton: Princeton University Press, 1961.
Contains some new material.

WILLIAM MAKEPEACE THACKERAY

by Laurence Brander

WILLIAM MAKEPEACE THACKERAY

From the portrait by Samuel Laurence in the National Portrait Gallery.
Reproduced by permission of the National Portrait Gallery.

William Makepeace Thackeray was born at Calcutta on July 18, 1811. He died in London on December 24, 1863.

THACKERAY

I. INTRODUCTION

WHEN the nineteenth century opened, the population of London was less than a million. By 1861, in Thackeray's last years, it was growing rapidly towards three millions. At the beginning of the century, immense docks were being built in the Thames estuary and new bridges were being thrown across the river. In the 'thirties and 'forties the railways came to London and the age of the post-chaise which Dickens loved to celebrate had come to an end.

The towns and villages which clustered round Westminster and the City became one unending sprawl, and the boroughs which then formed London were the greatest agglomeration of humanity ever known in the western world. All these people had to be entertained, and as many of them were well housed and had money to spare, publishers made it their business to make books and magazines fashionable. The age of Dickens and Thackeray was the age of reading. The average yearly number of new books rose from 850 between 1802 and 1807 to about 2,530 in 1853.

Everyone except the most serious-minded read novels. Scott had made the novel respectable. It offered entertainment and a pattern of living. A wonderful market was open to Dickens and Thackeray with the result that *Dombey and Son* and *Vanity Fair* were on sale at the same time in shilling parts. Dickens created a world of his own; a world essentially London which yet had never quite existed. Thackeray offered to his own Kensington and the new boroughs a picture of upper middle-class life in the ancient boroughs. In his own time they said he was a realist. Just after his death Bagehot wrote: 'A painfulness certainly clings like an atmosphere round Mr. Thackeray's writings, in consequence of his inseparable and ever-present realism.'

Thackeray drew a picture of the life and struggles of the rich and powerful middle class. He filled his books with the people of Bloomsbury and Mayfair and Kensington. He described their lives and their ideals so that they could enjoy the mirror, and so that suburbia could imitate them; and he did it because all his readers preferred that to anything else he offered them. Even while he was still producing the Pendennis novels, Bagehot wrote of Thackeray's suburban public: 'The delicate touches of our great satirist have, for such readers, not only the charm of wit, but likewise the interest of valuable information; he tells them of the topics which they want to know.'

Thackeray has many pleasures to offer. He can tell a story, *Barry Lyndon* and *Esmond*. He can make characters; no one more quickly and easily except Dickens; and Thackeray supplements the Dickens world with characters Dickens could never have drawn. Dickens could never have given us a mature man like Colonel Lambert, or a sophisticated one like Major Pendennis. Dickens's characters had quite remarkably undeveloped minds. For the same reason, Dickens could never have given us Becky or Beatrix or that most wonderful young woman, Ethel Newcome. The special pleasure Thackeray offers is that he can write. Again, so can Dickens. But not every English novelist writes well, and Thackeray could manage this difficult language, English, with most enviable skill.

He exercised his skill in two ways. He had a narrative style of weight and pace, best enjoyed in *Barry Lyndon*, *Vanity Fair* and *Esmond*, and developed in a special way in *The Virginians*. In *Denis Duval*, at the end, he uses a narrative style that is much more modern. The other style, which he used in the Pendennis series, was informal, conversational, diffuse. This was Thackeray himself; this, so far as technique is concerned, was his unique excellence. His early writing is good, well-paced narrative, with the ostentatious energy of Regency life. His writing in the golden decade, the fifties of last century, and just beyond it, is superb. Its secret was an easy yet disciplined colloquialism which makes it impossible to misread him when reading aloud. And reading aloud was a favourite Victorian pastime.

He could write and he was always writing. He had an endless gusto of creative energy. From the moment he lost his money as a young man, he wrote, and he never stopped writing till he died. 'As soon as a piece of work is out of hand,' he wrote in a late *Roundabout* paper, 'and before going to sleep, I like to begin another; it may be to write only half a dozen lines: but that is something towards Number the Next.'

II. THE LIFE

Thackeray's life was the material out of which the Pendennis
books, and much before them, was made. He was born in
Calcutta in 1811 and was brought home in 1816. He never
returned to India, so his knowledge of India and the Anglo-
Indian society of his time came from observing his family
and their connections. The dear old military men, for
example, who had served in the East India Company's
army came from his step-father and his friends. Thackeray's
father was a senior civilian in the Company's service, and
we can best glimpse him in a Chinnery drawing of the
Thackeray family when William was three. Richmond
Thackeray, the father, died in 1815, and the child was sent
home to school in the following year.

His mother stayed on in Calcutta to marry again, and
for the moment the focus must be on her. For what
happened to her when she was a teen-ager made so strong
an impression on Thackeray that it supplied one of the
themes which gave most energy to his satire in the great
novels. It was the theme of the marriage market and
the conduct of parents when finding husbands for their
daughters.

As a girl, Thackeray's mother had fallen in love with a
young officer, Captain Carmichael-Smyth. Her parents
disapproved, and when he had to go away they intercepted
his letters to her and lied to both of them. She was told he
had died, and he was told that she no longer wished to hear
from him. She was sent out to Calcutta where she married
Richmond Thackeray. One evening Richmond Thackeray
came home and told his wife there would be an additional
guest to dinner. He had met a most amusing officer down
from Agra and had invited him. The unexpected guest
arrived. It was Carmichael-Smyth. The shock was terrible
for both of them. After dinner they contrived to talk
privately and they realised how they had been duped. The
young officer returned forthwith to Agra. Eighteen months

after her husband's death Mrs. Thackeray married her first lover.

Meantime, Thackeray was unwillingly at school. When he left his first school and went to Charterhouse he still did not enjoy himself. Time and Cambridge eventually cured that unhappiness, and after Cambridge he made various false and rather dilettante attempts at finding a profession. The truth was that his father had left him too much money. He thought of art and of the law. He went to Paris to study art. There he fell in love, and as he lost his money at the same time, his fond step-father had to find a means of providing for him. He ingeniously bought a newspaper so that Thackeray could be appointed Paris correspondent and marry. The newspaper did not take long to fail, and then Thackeray found in his mother-in-law's behaviour a model for the Campaigner and Mrs. Baynes.

Soon the young couple were living in Bloomsbury, like the young people in *The Great Hoggarty Diamond* and in *Philip*. Children came, three daughters, of whom one died as a baby, and after the third was born, calamity. Mrs. Thackeray lost her reason and had to live with an attendant in the country. She outlived Thackeray, so he was condemned to a widower's life for ever. He had one sentimental friendship sufficiently deep to disturb him seriously, with Mrs. Brookfield. That story, with its abrupt termination, has now been fully told. Afterwards, as the two girls grew older, his life centred more and more on them.

A writer's domestic life is likely to be as simple as the life of the Vicar of Wakefield, who only moved from the blue bed to the brown. Thackeray moved from Bloomsbury to Kensington, where finally he built himself the lovely house in Palace Gardens which is now the Israeli Embassy. His life can be followed in the many portraits, drawings and photographs that were made of him, and the pictures and photographs of the rooms in which he wrote. He was a great friend of many artists, and was happy to live publicly in this way. By contrast, the intense privacy of a writer's life is seen in the Roundabout Papers, where the writer sits remembering and reflecting on paper. These papers are amongst the best autobiographical writing in the language and amongst the most revealing glimpses of the Victorian mind.

It was a good life, spent in energetic creation. He loved writing and he was always writing. He loved drawing and he was always drawing. He had an endless zest for creation and he came to his full fame and powers in the most glorious decade London has ever known, the fifties of last century. No great man in that society was a lonely eminence. Everyone of stature was surrounded by his peers. They lived to the full, hospitably and convivially. By the nature of his domestic loneliness, Thackeray depended more than most men on society. He spent his life in that ebullient society and in describing it.

After his death, Bagehot assessed Thackeray's contribution with his usual perceptiveness. Trollope, a little later, celebrated him sensibly and solidly in the English Men of Letters series. That book occasionally turns up in the second-hand bookshops and is well worth reading. The next notable assessment was by Saintsbury in his Introductions to the Oxford edition, which is especially useful in giving Thackeray's original and revised readings. Meanwhile, Gissing had introduced an effective comparison with Dickens in his book on Dickens; and a little later than all this, Chesterton produced a masterly short essay. All these tributes are by London bookmen on a great London bookman.

Contemporary work speaks for itself, but anyone writing on Thackeray will wish to acknowledge indebtedness to Professor Gordon Ray, whose sensible and sensitive devotion to Thackeray's work has produced all that the student can desire.

III. THE EARLY WORK AND *BARRY LYNDON*

For all his early works Thackeray used that popular medium the magazine. One or two of the journalists whom Thackeray met in his early newspaper days were, in the 'thirties, working for *Fraser's Magazine*. Mr. Fraser of Regent Street followed the fashion of the time in offering a monthly collection of stories, essays and travel pieces. There was much Improvement in the mixture, for Mr. Fraser had a Scottish tact in catering for his public. The earliest numbers were devoted to decorum, dullness, and the usual list of bankrupts. But the Magazine survived, and eventually Thackeray was employed to offer light relief, which he began to do in *The Yellowplush* papers in 1837-38. In the first year of Queen Victoria's reign the public taste, it would appear, was for robust, simple fun and Thackeray spiced his with a wit that darts, and strikes more than one target. Yellowplush in this sample is addressing his fellow-servants in their club just after they have discovered he is an author:

> 'I am,' says I, in a neat spitch, 'I am a littery man—there is no shame in it in the present instins; though, in general, its a blaggard employment enough. But it aint my *trade*—it isnt for the looker of gain that I sitt pen to payper—it is in the saycred caws of nollitch.' (*Hear, hear.*)

Equally extravagant, with a farcical extravagance which was for some time to be Thackeray's favourite Irish manner, was *Major Gahagan*, which appeared in the following year in *The New Monthly Magazine*, still edited by Theodore Hook. The literature of extravagance in English is delightful, and there is much amusement in this example. Major Gahagan has discovered that his beloved in the besieged town has none of her favourite elephant steak for supper. But outside lie the elephants the Major killed only a couple of days ago:

> I rushed out; not a single man would follow. The bodies of the elephants we had killed still lay on the ground where they had

fallen, about four hundred yards from the fort. I descended calmly the hill, a very steep one, and coming to the spot, took my pick of the animals, choosing a tolerably small and plump one, of about thirteen feet high, which the vultures had respected. I threw this animal over my shoulders, and made for the fort.

As I marched up the declivity, whizz—piff—whirr! came the balls over my head; and pitter-patter, pitter-patter they fell on the body of the elephant like drops of rain. The enemy were behind me; I knew it, and quickened my pace. I heard the gallop of their horse: they came nearer, nearer; I was within a hundred yards of the fort—seventy—fifty! I strained every nerve; I panted with superhuman exertion—I ran—could a man run very fast with such a tremendous weight on his shoulders?

Alas, the Major's efforts to provide a steak for his beloved's supper are made at the expense of his own safety. He drops in a faint as he shoves the elephant through the gate of the citadel: 'exhausted nature could bear no more.'

In the following year, 1839, *Catherine* appeared in *Fraser's*. It had the same energy of invention, in a very different mood, for it pretended to be a most serious exposure of crime stories popular at that time, and was in fact itself a very good one. It was the first of Thackeray's short novels, a kind in which he became expert. The story line was usually melodramatic, rising to a final scene when all the principal characters appear. *Catherine* was based on a particularly atrocious murder, which offered Thackeray a gruesome finale. The opening however is a village scene, soldiers and rustics on the village green, and for the first time Thackeray sketches rural England, as he was to do so often and so memorably. For the first time there is a plot, comparatively real characters, and a background that is perfectly real. The prose takes on colour and pace; the *tempo* of the story rises.

The technique is repeated a year later in *Fraser's* in *A Shabby Genteel Story*. The characters move and speak in the jerky way puppets have, but there is story interest, with a Cinderella heroine and a bogus young artist who is carried off in the end by a rich old woman who marries him. The prose is simple and speedy and that, like the youthfully hard story line, contrasts sharply with the note which Thackeray appended at the end of the 1857 reprint in his *Miscellanies*:

> When the republication of these Miscellanies was announced, it was my intention to complete the little story, of which only the first part is here written. Perhaps novel-readers will understand, even from the above chapters, what was to ensue. . . . The tale was interrupted at a sad period of the writer's own life. The colours are long since dry; the artist's hand is changed.

Between the writing of the story and the note, the Victorian Age had arrived.

In the next story, in the following year, there were affinities with his later work. In fact, *The Great Hoggarty Diamond* is in many ways an early version of the halcyon story in *Philip* of young married life in Bloomsbury. In its main theme, the rise and fall of Mr. Brough, the swindling financier, it is as harsh as any of the early short novels. It foreshadows a notable aspect of the Pendennis stories in having an overbearing female clouding and harassing the lives of the young people. An Irish aunt lives with them and on them, and generally deprives them of happiness. The dominant note is a welcome one, for it is a lyrical description of young married life, which is an autobiographical celebration. The whole business of learning to live, dealing with servants, entertaining, meeting the bills, these and the aura of happiness. In these pleasantly sentimental realistic descriptions Thackeray was never surpassed and here, in *The Great Hoggarty Diamond*, they first appear.

The most agreeable way to return to these early stories is by reading them in the four volumes of the *Miscellanies* which Thackeray himself collected in 1857, which were so often reprinted and which are still fairly easy to obtain. These volumes contain much more material than there has been room to discuss here, and most of it is still amusing to anyone who enjoys the harsh, male Regency spirit as well as the first buds of Victorian sentiment. There are readers who prefer these early stories to anything Thackeray wrote later, and certainly there are many who prefer them to the Thackeray of the Pendennis sequence, with its diffuse manner and its regular interruptions by the narrator as commentator and moralist.

Most of these early pieces are vigorous story-telling on the simple formula of having a beginning which quickly leads to a middle which hurries to a full-stage ending. They are full of villains, because villains are full of energy—and often generosity—which makes for good story-telling; not at all because villains can be preached about. In these early stories there is no preaching. They are simple, elementary narratives, sophisticated pleasantly with touches of satire:

> Yes, thank Heaven! there is about a freeborn Briton a cringing baseness and lick-spittle awe of rank, which does not exist under any tyranny in Europe, and is only to be found here and in America.

There are two more items in this collection of early material which must be noticed. First, the *Book of Snobs*, which appeared in *Punch* in 1846–47. Thackeray had been warned not to touch *Punch* when it first appeared in 1841. The warning was reasonable, and *Punch* failed to excite the market until Hood's *Song of a Shirt* appeared as a double page spread in the Christmas Number of 1843.

Thackeray ignored the advice. The *Snob* papers are the best of his contributions to *Punch*, and it is fair to say that along with Jerrold's *Mrs. Caudle's Curtain Lectures*, which appeared at the same time, they gave *Punch* the vitality which set it on its long career. One way of enjoying the *Snob* papers is to contrast them with *Boz*. In *Boz*, Dickens exploited very early his genius for describing a place and making it real and stereoscopic in our mind's eye. In the *Snob*, Thackeray exploited very early his satirical genius for bringing a character alive in a sentence and giving him identity in a page. The *Snob* papers are, most of them, brilliant sketches of London types, and can be enjoyed today because the same sort of people are going about awaiting the same critical attention.

The other item which must be noticed is the most important piece in the collection, *Barry Lyndon*, his first full-length novel. *Barry Lyndon* is well organised, and for those who like Thackeray the story-teller rather than Thackeray the diffuse creator of a society, it stands between the shorter novels and *Esmond*. Like them, it is taut story-telling. Indeed, apart from the last chapters, which tell the unbearable story of how Barry treated his wife and step-son, it is uncommonly good story-telling.

All the hints and suggestions contained in the sketches and the shorter novels are fused for the first time into a coherent point of view. *Barry Lyndon* is the last of his Regency pieces, though written in the next reign. Like the others, it would seem to be based on ridicule. But here, his characters are not ridiculous. They are noticeable figures in the European scene, and in all his work afterwards Thackeray was ready not only to reach back into the eighteenth century but to reach across to Western Europe. His great panoramas needed space as well as time; and it would seem that here he accepted the world as a Vanity Fair in which evil was the active, dominating spirit, and selfishness was the driving energy of the world.

Barry Lyndon was the last piece Thackeray published in magazine form until he contributed *Lovel the Widower* to his own *Cornhill* in 1860. In the next decade, the 'fifties, he wrote another series of shorter pieces which appeared in a new publishing format, the Christmas Book.

The Christmas Book replaced the Annual, which had been in favour during the 'thirties. Hood had extended the range of the Annuals in his famous Comic Annuals, and it was this tradition of Christmas gaiety which the publishers now exploited. Far and away the most famous of them is Dickens's *Christmas Carol*, and probably the only other Christmas Book popularly remembered is Thackeray's *Rose and the*

Ring. But Thackeray produced them regularly for some years, and we may couple them with his verses to illustrate the abundant fecundity of his genius.

Like many good prosemen, Thackeray, when he wrote verse, wrote light verse. When he wanted to express himself, he used prose. When he wanted to be gay, he might use prose or verse or make little drawings. Some of his verses, like *Little Bill-ee*, have become part of the delightful furniture of the English nursery mind. Otherwise, they have been forgotten.

So has another piece which once found favour. We live in an age when travel books are a favourite form of publishing and travel books of all times are enjoyed. But Thackeray's *Cornhill to Cairo* is almost and rightly forgotten. Like the Christmas books, it was in response to a popular publishing kind. Like them, it appeared in an attractive format, expensively illustrated. Only the strongest appetite for travel books can make it readable today.

IV. *VANITY FAIR*

There was another kind of publishing, which Dickens had used with great success, and which Thackeray, perhaps for that very reason, had not attempted. It was the fashion of producing a novel in shilling monthly parts. Thackeray used it at last for *Vanity Fair*, and as these monthly parts appeared, Thackeray, who already enjoyed a considerable though not an outstanding reputation as a writer, suddenly found himself famous.

It is his greatest work. Nothing before it is in anything like the same class in sweep and energy. After it came the Pendennis sequence and *Esmond*, but none of them challenge the creative glow and richness of *Vanity Fair*. It was as sudden as it was unrepeatable, and though Thackeray explored a hundred years back, and all the resources of his experience and personality, he never managed anything so powerful again.

The story moves steadily, even speedily, right from the start; and it was getting a story under way that Thackeray so often found difficult. The characters come alive at once, and they are all easy to meet. The prose is, at its best, easy but speedy. Salty too, for it carries neater, harder comments than anywhere else. Ridicule has given way to irony. The whole performance has brilliance and power so well under control that none of it is wasted.

He gathers into this novel all his special skills. All his life he wrote about London for Londoners and anyone else who cared to listen. He never wrote about it better than in this broad panorama. He was a maker of characters, and he never made characters more vividly real than he did here. He was an historical novelist, and nowhere else has he given so poignantly the sense of the moral desolation of war, which makes so much of human history. He painted portraits of London families, and the Osbornes and the Sedleys are amongst his most finished family portraits; they are certainly so in illustrating his private theme that the family and the household could conceal great cruelty, for which there is no discovery and no redress.

It is one of the few novels in which Thackeray is Olympian. In *Barry Lyndon* he is tough and satirical. In *Esmond* he becomes a great English aristocrat of the eighteenth century. In the Pendennis sequence he is a great contemporary personality to his first readers. But in *Vanity Fair* he has an Olympian impersonality, with only an occasional personal intrusion to sharpen the focus. Much later, in *The Virginians*, he does the same, at a critical point dropping the impersonal omniscience to tell the story personally and give the needed warmth of feeling.

Being an historical panorama, *Vanity Fair* had to be given shape and proportion. So it was written as a book, like *Esmond*, and not as a narrative stream, like the Pendennis books. Like all successful long novels, it is a series of scenes which follow one another not accidentally but as calculated contrasts, high life alternating with low, the tension of pain with the relaxation of comedy.

The scenes build up into the panorama effect which is secured by withdrawing the point of observation so that the focus broadens to take in the European scene at the time of Waterloo. Thackeray later gets a similar effect in *The Virginians*, when he is celebrating the youth of a people on a vast land mass. He is more certain in the earlier focus of *Vanity Fair*, and that certainty is, as always, a matter of time as well as space. He is writing of a time which his older friends had known and out of which he himself grew. The atmosphere of it was his birthright.

It is always so with the historical novelist; collective memory is truer than the greatest imaginative conception of earlier times. So *Vanity Fair* is more true than *Esmond* and *The Virginians*. It is not more true than the Pendennis novels, but it has this advantage, that its point in space-time gives it a unity and finality which the other great panoramic compositions lack because they merge into the present.

Among the characters the women are the most interesting,

and the contrast between Becky and Amelia is one of the most discussed subjects in English fiction. In a sense, Amelia is the stronger woman. Once or twice she becomes uncontrollably angry and at once gets what she wants. Becky, we notice, can fail in a crisis. She cannot prevent Rawdon from knocking Steyne down. On one occasion she gives way to selfless generosity, when she surprises Amelia out of her dreams and shows her how wrong she was to idolise the memory of George, how cruelly selfish she was being to Dobbin.

There was a moment, when Dobbin first returned from Madras, at which all could have gone well: It was his meeting with Amelia in Kensington Gardens:

> He looked at her—oh, how fondly—as she came running towards him, her hands before her, ready to give them to him. She wasn't changed. She was a little pale: a little stouter in figure. Her eyes were the same, the kind trustful eyes. There were scarce three lines of silver in her soft brown hair. She gave him both her hands as she looked up flushing and smiling through her tears into his honest homely face. He took the two little hands between his two, and held them there. He was speechless for a moment. Why did he not take her in his arms, and swear that he would never leave her? She must have yielded: she could not but have obeyed him.
>
> 'I—I've another arrival to announce,' he said, after a pause.
>
> 'Mrs. Dobbin?' Amelia said, making a movement back—Why didn't he speak?
>
> 'No,' he said, letting her hands go: 'Who has told you those lies?—I mean, your brother Jos came in the same ship with me, and is come home to make you all happy.'

The moment passed, and much happened before Becky, in a moment of good sense and generosity, settled the question. She is speaking to Amelia:

> '. . . You are no more fit to live in the world than a baby in arms. You must marry, or you and your precious boy will go to ruin. You must have a husband, you fool; and one of the best

gentlemen I ever saw has offered you a hundred times, and you have rejected him, you silly, heartless, ungrateful little creature!'

'I tried—I tried my best, indeed I did, Rebecca,' said Amelia, deprecatingly, 'but I couldn't forget . . .' and she finished the sentence by looking up at the portrait.

'Couldn't forget *him*!' cried out Becky, 'that selfish humbug, that low-bred cockney dandy, that padded booby, who had neither wit, nor manners, nor heart, and was no more to be compared to your friend with the bamboo cane, than you are to Queen Elizabeth. Why, the man was weary of you, and would have jilted you, but that Dobbin forced him to keep his word. He owned it to me. He never cared for you. He used to sneer about you to me, time after time; and made love to me the week after he married you.'

'It's false! It's false! Rebècca,' cried Amelia, starting up.

'Look there, you fool,' Becky said, still with provoking good humour, and taking a little paper out of her belt, she opened it and flung it into Emmy's lap. 'You know his handwriting. He wrote that to me—wanted me to run away with him—gave it me under your nose, the day before he was shot—and served him right!' Becky repeated.

Emmy did not hear her; she was looking at the letter. It was that which George had put into the bouquet and given to Becky on the night of the Duchess of Richmond's ball. It was as she said: the foolish young man had asked her to fly.

That is shock treatment of dramatic quality[1] and the woman who gives it is the outstanding character in the book. She is the most remarkable character in Thackeray's long series of female portraits. She is eternally energetic and always scheming. She is provocative, inspiring and dangerous as fire. Beatrix Esmond alone can stand beside her, and even Beatrix only rivals her by possessing the tragic quality of the mistress who is fatal to the men she loves.

The emotional pitch in *Vanity Fair* is higher throughout

[1] But see Mrs. Tillotson in *Novels of the Eighteen-Forties*, p. 244. 'Amelia has already relented and written to recall Dobbin. The inner necessity of the scene is rather to leave no sham unexposed.' It is also possible that but for Becky's candour Amelia might have hesitated at the last moment again.

than in any other Thackeray novel. It is only rivalled in the great *Esmond* scenes, as when Esmond returns from the wars to Lady Castlewood and Beatrix at Winchester. The prose is taut, as always in the pastiche of Esmond, and as in the great historical passages in *The Virginians*. All this combines to give *Vanity Fair* a richness of texture and a wealth of energy and colour which makes it a panoramic display without a rival in English fiction.

V. *ESMOND* AND *THE VIRGINIANS*

Vanity Fair opened up for Thackeray two lines of development. He could exploit his gift for painting the London scene; he could write historical novels. He did both. His next novel was *Pendennis;* and in that sequence, as it became, *The Newcomes* and *Philip* followed over a decade. After *Pendennis* he wrote *Esmond*, followed by *The Virginians*. In this, towards the end, there is a reference to Barry Lyndon, and the Warringtons make a link with *Pendennis*. By means of such links throughout his work, Thackeray built up a whole society.

Among the advantages of writing about former times, Thackeray exploited two. First, the composition has the completeness of a story of long ago, with everything finished and the values of the actions all decided. Second, real people of some fame in the world are introduced. Such characters are best on the fringe, and Thackeray in *Esmond* satisfies his dislike and contempt for Marlborough by showing his influence while hardly ever bringing him on the scene. In the same way, his view that the Stuarts were quite unequal to their opportunites of regaining their throne, and unworthy of their followers, can be best expressed by keeping the Pretender off stage as much as possible, though he is at the centre of a crisis late in the story. Both Marlborough and the Pretender are influences, great influences suitable to their rank, rather than characters.

The characters are the lesser aristocracy, of a rank and station high enough to give Thackeray a chance to develop tragic situations, but not so high that their actions and characters are so well known that they hamper his creative freedom.

The development of Beatrix in all her beauty and fatality is one of the great glories of English fiction. As a young girl, her irresponsible prattle leads to her father's death. As a woman, her actions lead to the death of the Duke she was going to marry. It is a portrait of an irresistibly beautiful woman who was cursed with a flaw in her nature which was fatal and unchangeable.

Her mother is in complete contrast, a mother type. In the beginning, she is like a mother to Esmond. Half-way through, when he makes a young man's profession of love to her, she insists on the mother relationship. At the end, when he has grown, and the few years between them have become as nothing, they marry. Meantime, between his first declaration and their confession of love and their marriage, Esmond is at the mercy of the beauty and cruelty of Beatrix.

Like the two women in *Vanity Fair*, these two are much more real than any of the men in the book. The story proceeds in its astonishing pastiche of eighteenth-century prose through the story of Castlewood and Mohun to the campaigns of Marlborough, and through an imaginary and abortive visit of the Pretender to London. The scene widens, as the boy Esmond grows into manhood, from the English countryside to London and to Europe.

The story is beautifully managed. The characters develop and live in the context of great events and everything that happens seems inevitable. The scenes in the great country house at the beginning, tinged with the sadness of remembrance of times long past and places far away; then the London scenes in Thackeray's Kensington, but a hundred and fifty years earlier; the battle pieces in Flanders and Esmond's return to find Beatrix grown and beautiful:

> Esmond had left a child and found a woman, grown beyond the common height; and arrived at such a dazzling completeness of beauty, that his eyes might well show surprise and delight at beholding her. In hers there was a brightness so lustrous and melting, that I have seen a whole assembly follow her as if by an attraction irresistible: and that night the great Duke was at the playhouse after Ramillies, every soul turned and looked (she chanced to enter at the opposite side of the theatre at the same moment) at her, and not at him. She was a brown beauty: that is, her eyes, hair, and eyebrows and eyelashes were dark: her hair curling with rich

undulations, and waving over her shoulders; but her complexion was as dazzling white as snow in sunshine: except her cheeks, which were bright red, and her lips, which were of a still deeper crimson. Her mouth and chin, they said, were too large and full, and so they might be for a goddess in marble, but not for a woman whose eyes were fire, whose look was love, whose voice was the sweetest low song, whose shape was perfect symmetry, health, decision, activity, whose foot as it planted itself on the ground was firm but flexible, and whose motion, whether rapid or slow, was always perfect grace—agile as a nymph, lofty as a queen—now melting, now imperious, now sarcastic—there was no single movement of hers but was beautiful. As he thinks of her, he who writes feels young again, and remembers a paragon.

This is the excitement and sentiment of Steele, and when Thackeray quotes one of his *Spectator* papers the texture of the prose does not change. To complete the eighteenth-century illusion, Thackeray had the early editions printed with the long eighteenth-century 's'. But the book was not popular. The public preferred the present they did not know to the past for which they cared nothing. Thackeray returned to his Pendennis stories, and when he did write a sequel to *Esmond* in *The Virginians* he seems to be thinking of his public in America.

In our remoter calculation there would seem to be one serious flaw in the book. Thackeray chooses to tell the story through a narrator who is at the centre of the story, and who is interested. In most ways that helps, because the central character, through whom we see these great events, is equal to describing and judging them. He can form a judgement on Marlborough and the Pretender as easily as on Dick Steele or his servant, John Lockwood.

All this gives the hero, the narrator, status. But he is interested. He takes sides. In the great historical judgements in the book, on Marlborough and on the Pretender, he is biased. The bias may have been Thackeray's. But if we compare this version of the conflict between Stuarts and Hanoverians with the version in Scott's *Waverley*, we see at once the advantage Scott enjoys by being the Olympian narrator. He can see the virtues on both sides. Vich Ian Vohr and Colonel Talbot are both heroic. Both command our admiration. The tragedy of the conflict is therefore heightened. The flaw in Esmond is that the Stuart Pretender never catches our sympathy, and never seems worth the trouble his followers took about him.

Esmond has a sequel in *The Virginians*. The atmosphere of Esmond is the English country house and the village attached to it, the neat little houses of eighteenth-century London and the Low Countries in rather stuffy weather. The atmosphere of *The Virginians* is the vast free air of America, with for contrast the cramped quarters of an almost *papier mâché* Tunbridge Wells.

The Virginians is a vast attempt. It describes the breaking away of a young nation from the parent. His generous picture of the young American people, with all the freshness of their honour and their seriousness about them, makes us sympathise with them and not with England. The Americans are given all that Thackeray thought became a man, the English all that is foolish and weak in the conduct of war and affairs of state.

This he could be sure would be enjoyed by readers on both sides of the Atlantic. Yet *The Virginians* fails to be real and convincing. It lacks the chemistry which turns make-believe into reality, that reality in a novel which is more intense than the run of our ordinary lives.

Thackeray in later life wanted to become an historian, to emulate Hume and Smollett and Macaulay. When he felt that his creative power was leaving him, the art of the historian would exercise his critical talent and that sensitive instrument his prose. The *Virginians* lies half way between *Vanity Fair* and the histories he never lived to write. For the finest thing in *The Virginians* is the sweep and strength of the historical opening.

When he died, he was writing *Denis Duval*, a fascinating fragment. His creative faculty has revived. His story-telling power has returned, but his prose is modified. Instead of depending markedly upon an eighteenth-century base, it is so modern it reminds us of the best of Stevenson. The setting is Winchelsea and Rye, and these ancient Channel towns are recreated for us in a mood which almost recalls Thomas Hardy. So in his last piece, Thackeray is moving towards the next generation of story-tellers.

The fragment appeared in *Cornhill* in 1864, posthumously. It did credit to his memory. There is no longer, as in the early stories, that passionate desire to write of evil which is a characteristic of the story-teller fixed forever in imma-turity. The story-teller in *Denis Duval* is in the second part of life, when the strands which hold society together are seen to be weak, and to need any strengthening they can get. "Virtue coheres, sin separates" is the theme which Dr. Bernard proposes again and again in this story, which in its unpretentious simplicity carries us back to the time before all the great novels, when Thackeray was providing regular amusement in the magazines.

VI. THE PENDENNIS SEQUENCE

One of the most obvious things about the Pendennis novels is Thackeray's refusal to use the tension of suspense, or his story-telling gift. In *Philip*, for example, to make quite sure of this at one point he says:

> I do not seek to create even surprises in this modest history, or condescend to keep candid readers in suspense about many matters which might possibly interest them. For instance, the matter of love has interested novel-readers for hundreds of years past, and doubtless will continue so to interest them. . . . Phil's first love affair, to which we are now coming, was a false start. I own it at once.

The marked quality of the Pendennis sequence is diffuseness. The reader is attracted by the writing, which is to say by the character of the narrator; and that character is what every novelist depends on in the end. The effect is panoramic, as in *Vanity Fair*, not as in that piece by calculated construction, but by a continuing sprawl of scenes and characters which are held together and become organic only by the loosest mechanism.

The abrupt changes of scene and the introduction of whole series of new characters were possible in the monthly part system, and how much Thackeray relied on that it is not possible to guess. The point is that he permitted himself to do so and produced triumphantly an imaginative world.

The narrator grows up in *Pendennis* and tells the story in *The Newcomes* and *Philip*. He is obviously a man in his forties and fifties, sympathetically looking back at his own youth, and just as sympathetically looking at young Clive Newcome and Philip. He is a charming Victorian gentleman of moderate means, happily married and almost uxorious, with his whole life based on his family and his writing. He is Thackeray himself, plus what Thackeray would have liked for himself. To some of us in London today, he might be the image of one of our friends.

In the Introduction to *Pendennis*, which he wrote after

the book was finished, Thackeray speaks of the novel as a
'sort of confidential talk'. This is an exact description of
the sequence. For the method is an extension of the essay
method, an essayist projecting his world through his personality.

It is an immensely rich world. It is the greatest panorama
of London life ever offered in a classic novel sequence. It
embraces the world as upper-class Londoners then enjoyed
it, from Kensington Gardens to Brighton, from Baden to
Rome. Thackeray was the sharp realist, and the Pendennis
world is a true picture of the world out of which London
now has grown. Bagehot expresses it well: 'The visible
scene of life—the streets, the servants, the clubs, the gossip,
the West End—fastened on his brain. These were to him
reality. They burnt in upon his brain; they pained his nerves;
their influence reached him through many avenues, which
ordinary men do not feel much, or to which they are
altogether impervious. He had distinct and rather painful
sensations where most men have but confused and blurred
ones.'

Pendennis is written on the Apprenticeship[1] pattern, a
Romantic pattern which gives the story of the writer's own
growth. In Dickens, *David Copperfield*. In some ways
Thackeray used the pattern better in *Philip*, for Philip
himself is drawn with more psychological depth and he is
more real and likeable than Pendennis. On the other hand,
it is a kind of novel in which good supporting characters
are necessary, and Pendennis has much better support than
Philip. The Victorians loved a crowded scene with active
vivid characters and *Pendennis* takes its place as one of the
great Victorian character collections.

The most engaging is the old soldier, Major Pendennis,
the only sophisticated old soldier Thackeray has given us.
The Major's handling of women and his management of
Pen's calf-love affair is the essential joy of the novel. The
sentimental feeling for the strolling players and Mr. Bowes,

[1] So named from Goethe's novel *Wilhelm Meister's Apprenticeship*.

and the harsh macabre Clavering characters provide piquant contrast. The Oxford scenes are not so good perhaps, for Thackeray went to the other place, but Foker is a jolly character and Warrington, the last of the Warringtons in Thackeray, carries about with him the family aura. Together, Foker and Warrington provide the necessary foils to the hero. It is a book without attractive women. Pen's mother is insipid, the Fotheringay is designed to be heavy on hand, Fanny Bolton is almost impossibly dim for Thackeray, and Blanche Amory is completely unattractive. Laura comes into her own later, as Mrs. Pendennis. It is a weakness of the plot that most of these women *have* to be unattractive, but the compensation is that there is a wealth of London characters, since the apprenticeship of Pendennis is a long and varied experience.

As with people, so with places. *Pendennis* gives us Warrington and Captain Shandon, and it also gives us their backgrounds in the Middle Temple and the Fleet Prison. They are all drawn to give his readers glimpses of their own city which they would never see for themselves and many of them are recalled from Thackeray's own apprenticeship, his apparently wasted youth. It is the world of *The Book of Snobs* and other earlier papers, presented with much less obvious ridicule and with what seems to us an excess of sentiment.

There is the same leaning towards sentiment in *The Newcomes*, which Thackeray built out of another part of his mental store, his recollections of his Anglo-Indian relations. Once again there is a splendid sufficiency of London sketches. The Cave of Harmony, the chambers in the Temple, the studios of the young painters, the dinners in the Squares. Once again there is a world of characters, the like of which the suburbs and posterity would never otherwise have known. Professional writers, Pendennis and Bayham; aristocrats, Kew and Jack Belsize; Anglo-Indians, the Colonel himself and the civilian, James Binnie; a fashionable preacher, Mr. Honeyman, with his Jewish backer, who promotes the parson as he would any other profitable performer. It is a book in which the minor characters are sharp in recollection, firm, gritty, real. They hold the interest, from James Binnie and the sweet Miss Honeyman to the Campaigner.

The two outstanding characters are the Colonel and Ethel. Both are studies of goodness, and characters with this quality are not only difficult to make interesting, they are difficult to make at all. Fairly early in the story, Thackeray found himself in difficulties over the Colonel and packed him off back to India. Later, he returns to be the foil to his banker relations, who typify the general closeness of the Victorian money world. The Colonel goes into their banking world, fails egregiously and retains his integrity and his goodness. Thackeray loved these retired soldiers, so like his step-father, who had an eccentricity based on native gentleness and an atrabilious fieriness nourished under the Indian sun.

Before the crash, Colonel Newcome is a fighting champion for the young people. When Barnes Newcome tells lies to keep Ethel and Clive apart 'the cup of Thomas Newcome's wrath overflowed. Barnes had lied about Ethel's visit to London; Barnes had lied in saying that he delivered the message with which his uncle charged him; Barnes had lied about the letter which he had received, and never sent. With these accusations firmly proven in his mind against his nephew, the Colonel went down to confront that sinner'. He found him in his bank:

'This young gentleman is one of your clerks?' asked Thomas Newcome, blandly.

'Yes; Mr. Boltby, who has your private account. This is Colonel Newcome, Mr. Boltby,' says Sir Barnes, in some wonder.

'Mr. Boltby, brother Hobson, you heard what Sir Barnes Newcome said just now respecting certain intelligence, which he grieved to give me?'

At this all three gentlemen respectively wore looks of amazement.

'Allow me to say in your presence, that I don't believe one single word Sir Barnes Newcome says, when he tells me that he is very sorry for some intelligence he has to communicate. He lies, Mr. Boltby; he is very glad. I made up my mind that in whatsoever company I met him, and on the very first day I found him—hold your tongue, sir; you shall speak afterwards and tell more lies when I have done—I made up my mind, I say, that on the very first occasion I would tell Sir Barnes Newcome that he was a liar and a cheat. He takes charge of letters and keeps them back. Did you break the seal, sir? There was nothing to steal in my letter to Miss Newcome. He tells me people are out of town whom he goes to see in the next street, after leaving my table, and whom I see myself half an hour after he lies to me about their absence.'

'Damn you, go out, and don't stand staring there, you booby!' screams out Sir Barnes to the clerk. 'Stop, Boltby. Colonel Newcome, unless you leave this room I shall—I shall——'

'You shall call a policeman. Send for the gentleman, and I will tell the Lord Mayor what I think of Sir Barnes Newcome, Baronet. Mr. Boltby, shall we have the constable in?'

'Sir, you are an old man, and my father's brother, or you know very well I would——'

'You would what, sir? Upon my word, Barnes Newcome' (here the Colonel's two hands and the bamboo cane came from the rear and formed in front), 'but that you are my father's grandson, after a menace like that, I would take you out and cane you in the presence of your clerks. I repeat, sir, that I consider you guilty of treachery, falsehood, and knavery. And if ever I see you at the Bay's Club, I will make the same statement to your acquaintance at the west end of the town. A man of your baseness ought to be known, sir; and it shall be my business to make men of honour aware of your character. Mr. Boltby, will you have the kindness to make out my account? Sir Barnes Newcome, for fear of consequences which I shall deplore, I recommend you to keep a wide berth of me, sir.' And the Colonel twirled his mustachios, and waved his cane in an ominous manner, and Barnes started back spontaneously out of its dangerous circle.

But Thackeray is a realist and in the end the Colonel goes down and Barnes flourishes.

The Colonel is still more sympathetic in adversity. When he comes home to tell his family that he has lost all his money and is about to be declared bankrupt, the scene opens thus:

> 'Has it come, Father?' said Clive, with a sure prescience, looking in his father's face.
>
> The father took and grasped the hand which his son held out. 'Let us go back into the dining-room,' he said. They entered it, and he filled himself a glass of wine out of the bottle still standing amidst the dessert. He bade the butler retire, who was lingering about the room and sideboard, and only wanted to know whether his master would have dinner, that was all. And, this gentleman having withdrawn, Colonel Newcome finished his glass of sherry and broke a biscuit; the Campaigner assuming an attitude of surprise and indignation, whilst Rosey had leisure to remark that Papa looked very ill, and that something must have happened.

The vulgar outcries of the two women follow and when they have gone, the scene ends thus:

> 'Here's a good end to it,' says Clive, with flashing eyes and a flushed face, 'and here's a health till to-morrow, Father!' and he filled into two glasses the wine still remaining in the flask. 'Goodbye to our fortune, and bad luck go with her—I puff the prostitute away— *Si celeres quatit pennas*, you remember what we used to say at Grey Friars—*resigno quae dedit, et mea virtute me involvo, probamque pauperiem sine dote quaero*.' And he pledged his father, who drank his wine, his hand shaking as he raised the glass to his lips, and his kind voice trembling as he uttered the well-known old school words, with an emotion that was as sacred as a prayer. Once more, and with hearts full of love, the two men embraced.

They fell back instinctively on their training and behaved well. This is a glimpse of the generations which Thackeray loved to give, the other side of the Victorian medal from *Father and Son* and *The Way of All Flesh*. It is on a par with Philip's loyalty to his father. It is the pristine brightness of family honour preserved in the actions and demeanour of the young.

In Ethel, Thackeray had his greatest success in portraying a heroine. Her character developed in opposition to the mercenary outlook of her family. She is a portrait of a natural aristocrat; she is all that the upper middle classes could have wished to be. We feel that she is the counterpart of the Colonel, and that when she at last marries Clive (we hear casually in *Philip* that they did marry) she will make as fine a man of him as his father was. Goodness is a quality that is apt to turn into something else while it is being described. Thackeray overcame the difficulty simply. He presents Ethel to us by the simple means of letting us see her through other eyes. For example, through the eyes of Laura Pendennis, whose judgement on women we trust as much as Pendennis did himself. Or through the eyes of Pendennis and the old family solicitor in this typical Victorian novel scene of joy and salvation through splendid generosity with money. Ethel has discovered that a great part of the money she has inherited should have gone to Clive in justice though not in law. Without hesitation she demands of her brother Barnes that her grandmother's wish be honoured. They quarrel because he refuses, and she asks Pendennis to take her to the family solicitor. It is her nature not to rest until the thing is put right:

'. . . I consulted with this gentleman, the husband of my dearest friend, Mrs. Pendennis—the most intimate friend of my uncle and cousin Clive; and I wish, and I desire and insist, that my share of what my poor father left us girls should be given to my cousin, Mr. Clive Newcome, in accordance with my grandmother's dying wishes.'

'My dear, you gave away your portion to your brothers and sisters ever so long ago!' cried the lawyer.

'I desire, sir, that six thousand pounds may be given to my cousin,' Miss Newcome said, blushing deeply. 'My dear uncle, the best man in the world, whom I love with all my heart, sir, is in the most dreadful poverty. Do you know where he is, sir? My dear, kind, generous uncle!'—and, kindling as she spoke, and with eyes beaming a bright kindness, and flushing cheeks, and a voice that thrilled to the heart of those two who heard her, Miss Newcome went on to tell of her uncle's and cousin's misfortunes, and of her wish, under God, to relieve them. I see before me now the figure of the noble girl as she speaks; the pleased little lawyer, bobbing his white head, looking up at her with his twinkling eyes—patting his knees, patting his snuff-box—as he sits before his tapes and his deeds, surrounded by a great background of tin boxes.

'And I understand you want this money paid as coming from the family, and not from Miss Newcome?' says Mr. Luce.

'Coming from the family—exactly'—answers Miss Newcome.

Mr. Luce rose up from his old chair—his worn-out old horsehair chair—where he had sat for half a century and listened to many a speaker very different from this one. 'Mr. Pendennis,' he said, 'I envy you your journey along with this young lady. I envy you the good news you are going to carry to your friends—and, Miss Newcome, as I am an old—old gentleman who has known your family these sixty years, and saw your father in his long-clothes, may I tell you how heartily and sincerely I—I love and respect you, my dear? When should you wish Mr. Newcome to have his legacy?'

'I think I should like Mr. Pendennis to have it this instant, Mr. Luce, please,' said the young lady.

These two characters, Ethel and the Colonel, stand out, and the scenes in which they appear stand out in a general level of performance which is too relaxed to be as uniformly amusing as Pendennis. There is just a thought at times that for lack of interest in the characters he has got on his hands, Thackeray calls up a world of new ones to see if they are any more amusing. He is competent always; he is always dexterous, and whenever necessary he displays the virtuosity of the professional performer. In the end, there can be no quarrelling with a novel that gives us characters like Ethel and Colonel Newcome and old Lady Kew, or scenes like the old Anglo-Indians' dinner party in Clifford Street, Mr. Honeyman preaching, the studios of the young artists and the auctioning of all the Colonel's splendour. There are moments in *The Newcomes* which we remember as we remember all moments of especially percipient understanding. One of them is when young Lord Kew releases Ethel after she has shown him the letter:

When he saw Ethel again, which he did in an hour's time, the generous young gentleman held his hand out to her. 'My dear,' he said, 'if you had loved me you never would have shown me that letter.' It was his only reproof. After that he never again reproved or advised her.

He knew whom Ethel loved, but we are no more sure than in real life whether Ethel knew herself. Not many novelists have that quality of realism, and our enjoyment of the English novel is incomplete if we have missed *The Newcomes*.

Of the trilogy which forms the Pendennis sequence, *Philip* is the weakest; but its reputation is much lower than it deserves, probably because of the very poor opening chapters. Thackeray had long been unwell, and when he took over the *Cornhill* in 1860, he had hoped to have *Philip* ready for serial use. When it came to the point he only had that strange performance, *Lovel the Widower*, and had to coax Anthony Trollope to fill the place of *Philip* with *Framley Parsonage*.

The interest of *Philip*, after the slow, weak opening, is that it is a development of the Pendennis autobiographical disclosures. The old man is commenting freely and sadly on his own youth. It is a classical *locus* in the English novel of our wincing memories of youthful incidents. Later on it takes us right back to *The Great Hoggarty Diamond* in being a celebration of young love and early married life.

Thackeray never made a gentler hero nor one who suffered so much. Philip's nerves are jangling all the time and the narrator at times is hardly in better case. At moments it almost seems that too much watching of this London Vanity Fair was driving the observer mad. 'The atmosphere of those polite drawing-rooms stifles me. I can't bow the knee to the horrible old Mammon. I walk about in the crowds as lonely as if I was in a wilderness. . .' It is Philip, not Pendennis, speaking there but it is also Thackeray. Philip's nostalgic gentleness saves him, just as it helps him to endure his father.

Philip in this matter is a precursor of the later Victorian pictures of unhappy father–son relationships, by Samuel

Butler and Edmund Gosse. But the psychology is different. Philip begins as an Angry Young Man, but he rapidly develops and becomes generous, and nothing that his father does can embitter the gentleness of his spirit.

The novel begins weakly and for three chapters is grey and thin. Suddenly, in Chapter Four, the old Thackeray virtuosity reappears, and the diffuse, entrancing monologue is on. Love at first sight in Boulogne, the quarrel of the old officers in the dreary *pension* in Paris, the narrator's own domestic background and the fury of the mother-in-law. Have these things been bettered in Thackeray or elsewhere? We are ready to enjoy the paintings of Frith these days, and we adore a crinoline. The whole Victorian age, maho-gany by gaslight, is engaging our willing attention. Shall we continue to neglect these Pendennis novels which are a reservoir of the most subtle imaginative prose writing of the 'fifties?

The pleasures that we find there are the pleasures that we value in life; humour and urbanity, based on security. For behind the personal misfortunes which make the plots is a perfectly secure social structure moving with glacial slow-ness towards inevitable betterment.

VII. *CORNHILL* AND THE LECTURES

Thackeray was a bad editor. He was too kind, and the office work bored him. But his name gave *Cornhill* an immense impetus, so that it started with the phenomenal sale of 110,000, which shows what an avid public the publishers had made in London during Thackeray's lifetime. Thackeray's personal contribution was first of all the second serial, *Lovel the Widower*, and then *Philip*. After his death there was *Denis Duval*, but far better than any of these were *The Roundabout Papers*, in which he exploited so well those gifts as an essayist which are indicated in the Pendennis books.

Lovel the Widower is a pale performance, but it has quite exceptional interest for the student of Thackeray. Everyone in the story is improbable and so are the incidents. The story line is similar to the one used in so many early Thackeray long-short stories, a gentle build-up to a final dramatic scene. The special interest is the heroine. In her we see Thackeray going as far as he dare in faithfully showing the nature of a strongly-sexed woman. She is a governess in a widower's family in an expensive Putney household. She has that fatal attraction which affects all the men around her, the butler, the apothecary, the narrator and her master. Needless to say, she chooses her master, who unexpectedly declares himself in the classic comic situation, when she is just going to be sent packing by his mother and mother-in-law. This is a curious counterpart of the normal satirising of the Victorian marriage market. Never does he show such heartless calculation as in this girl who looks after herself without a moment's thought for any of her victims. The story line is a powerful one, but the actual telling is weak. The reader feels, as in the opening of *Philip*, that the writer is ill, and the performance lacks stereoscopic reality.

If the late novels were a sort of confidential talk, the lectures were all that was formal in public speaking.

Thackeray went out lecturing because he wanted to leave plenty of money to his two daughters. Dickens had been wonderfully successful with his readings, why should Thackeray not cash in on the popular desire in Britain and America to see and hear the popular writer?

He prepared *The English Humourists* first. They have very little value to the student today though Thackeray made no mistake about who were the best eighteenth-century writers. But his view on the eighteenth century and ours are poles apart, and if his lectures are read with appreciation at all today it will be by the professional lecturer. They are a model for the presentation of a literary subject to a philistine audience. He knew that he had to presume complete ignorance. He began with Swift, and quoted Swift for comparison when he came to Steele, and both when he came to Addison and so on, comparing and at the same time reminding.

His method is to tell the story of these writers' lives and to draw their characters. The common reader loves it, as Somerset Maugham has been showing us today. By using this technique, Thackeray was able to quote from his authors without alarming his audience. It was an ideal way of giving a popular audience as much as it could comfortably digest. When it came to printing them, he extended the anthology in the text by adding copious quotations as footnotes. Simple and agreeable, but today these lectures are only interesting for what they tell us about the lecturer.

The Four Georges were prepared originally for American consumption and in them he develops a point of view in courteous deference to his audience. His views are those with which we are familiar in *Barry Lyndon* and *The Virginians*. None of these lectures is much read now, although they enjoyed a long success in book form. They certainly cannot be recommended to students of the eighteenth century.

By contrast, *The Roundabout Papers* are still excellent reading. In the great days of their mature reputations, both Dickens and Thackeray had forums from which they could speak to their readers. Dickens wrote *The Uncommercial Traveller* in *All the Year Round* and Thackeray *The Roundabout Papers* in *Cornhill*. Each took the opportunity in these periodical essays of writing an occasional lay sermon. Dickens produced some savagely true and stern denunciations of Victorian life, while Thackeray's mood was different. He fought the evil that he saw through compassion. In an essay called *On a Chalk-mark on the Door* he talks about the servants, the people whose lives had haunted him ever since his first writings in the *Yellowplush* papers. Here, we have the nearest Thackeray got to the shame Victorians felt about the two nations in England:

> I am not going into the horrid old question of 'followers.' I don't mean cousins from the country, love-stricken policemen, or gentlemen in mufti from Knightsbridge Barracks; but people who have an occult right on the premises; the uncovenanted servants of the house; grey women who are seen at evening, with baskets flitting about area-railings; dingy shawls which drop you furtive curtseys in your neighbourhood; demure little Jacks who start up from behind boxes in the pantry. Those outsiders wear Thomas's crest and livery, and call him 'Sir'; those silent women address the female servants as 'Mum', and curtsey before them, squaring their arms over their wretched lean aprons. Then, again, those *servi servorum* have dependants in the vast, silent, poverty-stricken world outside your comfortable kitchen fire, in the world of darkness, and hunger, and miserable cold, and dank flagged cellars, and huddled straw, and rags, in which pale children are swarming.

In another Roundabout paper he sums up all his attempts and desires as a writer. Here is the spirit behind *Barry Lyndon* and *Henry Esmond* and *Denis Duval*, and the spirit behind the Pendennis books: 'If the gods would give me the desire of my heart, I should be able to write a story which boys would relish for the next few dozen centuries. The boy-critic loves the story: grown up, he loves the author who wrote the story.' Could there be a neater explanation of the

Thackeray *œuvre*? Or a prouder mock repentance than this? '. . . perhaps of all the novel-spinners now extant, the present speaker is the most addicted to preaching. Does he not stop perpetually in his story and begin to preach to you?. . . I cry *peccavi* loudly and heartily.' Whatever we may feel about the preaching in the novels, we all enjoy these *Roundabout Papers* and each of us can name his favourites. The Victorians, when we come to think of it, were not usually intimate writers. Anyone who wishes to meet intimately one of the finest Victorian minds could hardly do better than read *The Roundabout Papers*.

VIII. CONCLUSION

If a writer produces an *œuvre*, he may be expected to produce a point of view. Thackeray, the realist, the satirist, the commentator, could not fail to do so. But his point of view as shown in his fiction is limited and confined. He lived and worked through the worst of the Industrial Revolution. During his lifetime space and time were being contracted in England by the railways. The troubles of the north came more quickly south. He lived through the Oxford Movement and the scientific revolution marked usually by *The Origin of Species*. His great decade was also the decade of the Crimean War and the Indian Mutiny. We search his writings in vain for any mention of these things. Not that there was any social inhibition about any of these subjects. There were novelists then as now who could not escape being involved, men like Disraeli and Kingsley. But Thackeray, concerned with the secular problems, did not trouble to focus contemporary events.

He honoured his contract as a novelist by writing of personal and family relationships with a highly developed historical sense. The reader feels not only that he is following the fortunes of the Esmonds and Warringtons through the generations, but watching how each generation honoured its responsibilities towards society and passed them on to the next. It is this quality in the Thackeray panorama which gives it moral quality and depth.

There is nothing of this in the early brilliance of the Regency short novels. There is very little of it in *Barry Lyndon*, which is a mature work in giving us a sense of the unity of western Europe. It is first developed in *Vanity Fair*, and the success of *Vanity Fair* gave him hope. But very soon he was cribbed, cabined and confined by the conventions of his age. He published *Pendennis*, and as soon as it was completed he commented in the preface:

> Since the author of *Tom Jones* was buried, no writer of fiction among us has been permitted to depict to his utmost power a

MAN. We must drape him, and give him a certain conventional simper. Society will not tolerate the Natural in our Art.

In his next book, *Esmond*, he tried history again, offering a maturity and breadth of judgement which is only surpassed by the now neglected Scott. Both *Esmond* and *The Virginians* give a picture of a responsible society with values which were those out of which the values of Thackeray's own upper middle class had developed. For Esmond, Wolfe and Lambert are the men we are invited to admire, and whose like we long for in the leadership of the nation. Since *Esmond* was a comparative failure with his public, he returned in *The Newcomes* and *Philip*, as a professional writer must, to what his public expected of him. He gave up the splendours of moral judgement on great historical scenes and figures. He returned to the domestic scene, with the snob appeal of the upper middle classes and the spice of satire. He did what he was allowed to do, he criticised society within the conventions of his public. Since his greatest work is written near the 'fifties or in them, the golden decade of the English upper middle classes to which he belonged, his 'criticism' may be expected to be a celebration of the virtues that class most reverenced.

It is in fact so. In *Vanity Fair*, it is virtue and generosity of spirit which are shown to be most potent. In the context of *Vanity Fair*, where the characters pursue their selfish ends, the human condition is shown to be man at the mercy of his desires, and society a compact of mutually tolerated selfishness; sudden uncalculated moments of generosity or blazing virtue change the course of the story. These generous moments are paid for in *Vanity Fair*, but they have the power that goes with truth and generous thought and action.

Thackeray goes further back, into his beloved eighteenth century, to give us characters of steady, unfaltering virtue, who form that core of society which carries it forward. Not the establishment, which is a compromise with the way of the world, the grand committee of top people in *Vanity Fair*, but the individual virtuous man, celebrated in

European thinking by the Romans and always since. In Thackeray, men like Colonel Esmond and Colonel Lambert. They are men of integrity and quality who never compromise with evil.

These men were in no sense in opposition, they were apart. Opposition in Thackeray, opposition being that stress in human society which keeps it vital, is between the middle and lower classes. And the lower classes in Thackeray's novels are the servants. In their own way, they criticise and influence; they are always there, observing. Of the vast army of mechanics and labourers who followed Methodism and Charles Dickens, Thackeray knows nothing. It is all completely outside his imaginative world.

But from the beginning, he is intensely conscious of this opposition in society. The *Yellowplush* papers show it and it is present in *Vanity Fair* and *Pendennis*. Indeed, the nearest thing to social revolution and chaos in Thackeray is the revolt of Major Pendennis's man and the occupation of the Rawdon's flat by the servants who own it. In Thackeray's almost impregnable middle-class society, that is the only crack. A servant becoming rich by exploiting his careless master and using the power of his wealth in a vulgar way.

In that great portrait of an age, the Pendennis novels, we have Thackeray's mature and settled view of the society which he observed, He has no doubts about its power and its quality. It will go on for ever; that is in the nature of things. It will be compact of evil, and there will be generous, lovely people who will suffer and often survive and sometimes prevail. Neither good nor evil is confined to any stratum of society and there is no more likelihood of finding virtue in one stratum than another.

In *Denis Duval* comes the last word on these social questions. Evil destroys society. Virtue builds it and holds it together. That is completely commonplace; but when Thackeray adumbrates it in the texture of his mature narrative prose, it becomes moving and exciting again.

Since Thackeray's time our views have been modified. We are no longer certain that the upper middle classes and their beliefs will go on for ever because they are in the nature of things. We are at that stage in a social revolution when nearly everything is in doubt. So it is the middle classes who now return to Thackeray; for he painted their portrait in their hey-day.

But for all of us, Thackeray, in the normal course of his business as a professional writer, provides the best portrait we have of the class that was ruling England a hundred years ago. He observes the human scene with amusement and with the regard of a complete man, with the full range between the sentimental and the satirical. Like so many of the great men in that brilliantly rich generation, he could look at the human condition without despair.

WILLIAM MAKEPEACE THACKERAY

Select Bibliography

BIBLIOGRAPHIES

VAN DUZER, H. S. *A Thackeray Library*. New York: Priv. Ptd., 1910.
There is a long bibliography in Lewis Melville, *William Makepeace Thackeray*, 1910—see below.

Note. A full, definitive bibliography remains a desideratum. There are important Thackeray collections, which have been catalogued, at Princeton (Parrish Collection) and in the New York Public Library (Berg Collection).

COLLECTED EDITIONS

Miscellanies: Prose and Verse. 4 vols. London: Bradbury, 1854–1857; reprinted 1861 and 1865.
Vol. I includes *The Book of Snobs* and *Major Gahagan*; Vol. II, *The Memoirs of Mr. Yellowplush, Novels by Eminent Hands*; Vol. III, *The Memoirs of Barry Lyndon, A Legend of the Rhine, Rebecca and Rowena*; Vol. IV, *The Fitz-Boodle Papers, A Shabby Genteel Story, The Great Hoggarty Diamond*. The selection, made by Thackeray himself, provides the most convenient introduction to his early writings.

The Works. The Library Edition. 22 vols. Smith, Elder, 1874–1876.

Works. With a Memoir by Sir L. Stephen. 26 vols. 1878–1886.

Works. The Oxford Edition. 17 vols. London: Oxford University Press, 1908.
Introductions by G. Saintsbury. With original and revised readings, and additional material.

Works. The Centenary Biographical Edition. 26 vols. New York: Harper, 1910–1911.
Biographical introductions by Anne Thackeray Ritchie. These are useful and are profusely embellished with Thackeray's drawings. Includes Sir L. Stephen's Memoir.

Note. There are other collected editions, notably those edited by
H. E. Scudder (22 vols. Boston, 1889); edited by W. Jerrold (30 vols.
1901-1903); edited by 'L. Melville' (20 vols. 1901-1907; 1911).

LETTERS

The Letters and Private Papers. Collected and edited by Gordon N. Ray.
4 vols. Cambridge: Harvard University Press, 1945-1946.

SEPARATE WORKS

Dates of first London editions are given, and modern editions and
current paperbacks are also recorded here.

The Professor: A Tale, 1837.
First published in *Bentley's Miscellany*, 1837.

Memoirs of Mr. C. J. Yellowplush with *The Diary of C. Jeames de la Pluche,
Esqr.*, 1856.
First published in *Fraser's Magazine*, 1837-1838, as *The Yellowplush
Correspondence*.

Some Passages in the Life of Major Gahagan, 1838-1839.
First published in the *New Monthly Magazine*, 1838-1839.

Catherine: A Story. By Ikey Solomons, Esq., 1839-1840.
First published in *Fraser's Magazine*, 1839-1840.

Stubb's Calendar: Or, The Fatal Boots, 1839.
First published in *Cruikshank's Comic Annual*, 1839.

The Bedford Row Conspiracy, 1840.
First published in *New Monthly Magazine*, 1840.

The Paris Sketch Book. By Mr. Titmarsh. 2 vols. 1840.

A Shabby Genteel Story. New York, 1857.
First published in *Fraser's Magazine*, 1840.

An Essay on the Genius of George Cruikshank, 1840.
First published in the *Westminster Review*, 1840.

Barber Cox and the Cutting of His Comb, 1840.
First published in *Cruikshank's Comic Annual*. "Cox's Diaries" in the
Miscellanies.

The Great Hoggarty Diamond. New York, 1848.
First published in *Fraser's Magazine*, 1841.

The Second Funeral of Napoleon . . . and the Chronical of the Drum, 1841.

The Fitz-Boodle Papers, 1852.
First published in *Fraser's Magazine*, 1842-1843.

Miss Tickletoby's Lectures on English History, 1852.
  First published in *Punch*, 1842.

The Confessions of George Fitzboodle, 1843.
  First published in *Fraser's Magazine*, 1843. Reprinted with *The Fitz-Boodle Papers*, 1852.

The Irish Sketch-Book. By M. A. Titmarsh. 2 vols. 1843.

Bluebeard's Ghost. By M. A. Titmarsh, 1843.
  First published in *Fraser's Magazine*, 1843.

The Luck of Barry Lyndon: A Romance of the Last Century. By Fitz-Boodle.
  2 vols. New York, 1852. *Novel*.
  First·published in *Fraser's Magazine*, 1844. Revised as *The Memoirs of Barry Lyndon, Esq.* (1856). Edited by R. Morris (Lincoln: University of Nebraska Press, 1962).

A Legend of the Rhine. By Michael Angelo Titmarsh, 1845.
  First published in *George Cruikshank's Table-Book*, 1845.

Jeames's Diary: Or, Sudden Wealth. New York, 1846.
  First published in *Punch*, 1845–1846, as *Jeames's Diary*.

Proposals for a Continuation of "Ivanhoe," 1846.
  First published in *Fraser's Magazine*. Revised as *Rowena and Rebecca* (1850)—see below.

Notes of a Journey from Cornhill to Grand Cairo. By M. A. Titmarsh, 1846.

The Book of Snobs, 1848; complete edition, New York, 1852.
  First published in *Punch*, 1846–1847, as *The Snobs of England*.

Vanity Fair: A Novel Without a Hero, 1847–1848. *Novel*.
  First published in twenty monthly parts, January 1847–July 1848. Edited by G. and K. Tillotson (Riverside Edition).

Mrs. Perkin's Ball. By M. A. Titmarsh, 1847.

A Little Dinner at Timmins's, 1848.
  First published in *Punch*, 1848.

"Our Street." By Mr. M. A. Titmarsh, 1848.

The History of Pendennis. His Fortunes and Misfortunes. His Friends and His Greatest Enemy. 2 vols. 1849–1850. *Novel*.
  First published in twenty-four monthly parts, November 1848–December 1850.
  Everyman's Library, 2 vols.

Doctor Birch and His Young Friends. By Mr. M. A. Titmarsh, 1849.

Rebecca and Rowena: A Romance Upon Romance. By Mr. M. A. Titmarsh, 1850.

The Kickleburys on the Rhine. By Mr. M. A. Titmarsh, 1850.

The History of Henry Esmond, Esqre: A Colonel in the Service of Her Majesty Q. Anne. Written by Himself. 3 vols. 1862. *Novel.* Edited by G. N. Ray (Modern Library); Everyman's Library; Nelson Classics; Washington Square Paperback.

The English Humourists of the Eighteenth Century, 1853.
A series of lectures delivered in Great Britain and the U.S.A.

The Newcomes: Memoirs of a Most Respectful Family. Edited by Arthur Pendennis, Esqre. 2 vols. 1854–1855; revised, 1863. *Novel.*
First published in twenty-four monthly parts, October 1853–August 1855.
Everyman's Library, 2 vols.

Ballads, 1855.

The Rose and the Ring: Or, The History of Prince Giglio and Prince Bulbo. A Fireside Pantomime for Great and Small Children. By Mr. M. A. Titmarsh, 1855.
A facsimile by G. N. Ray of the original manuscript in the Morgan Library (New York: Pierpont Morgan Library, 1947); Nelson Classics.

The Virginians: A Tale of the Last Century. 2 vols. 1858–1859. *Novel.*
First published in twenty-four monthly parts, November 1857–September 1859.
Everyman's Library, 2 vols.

Lovel the Widower, 1861. *Novel.*
First published in the *Cornhill Magazine,* 1860.

The Four Georges: Sketches of Manners, Morals, Court and Town Life. New York, 1860; London, 1861.

Roundabout Papers, 1863.
First published in the *Cornhill Magazine,* 1860–1863.

The Adventures of Philip on His Way Through the World. 3 vols. 1862. *Novel.*
First published in the *Cornhill Magazine,* 1861–1862.

Denis Duval. New York, 1864; London, 1867. *Novel.*
First published in the *Cornhill Magazine,* 1864. Published posthumously.

BIOGRAPHICAL AND CRITICAL STUDIES

TROLLOPE, ANTHONY. *Thackeray*. English Men of Letters. New York: Harper, 1879.
Almost as useful on Thackeray as it is on Trollope.

WHIBLEY, C. *W. M. Thackeray*. New York: Dodd, Mead, 1903.
Sensitive, but marks the beginning of the critical revolt.

WILSON, JAMES G. *Thackeray in the United States, 1852–3, 1855–6*. 2 vols. New York: Dodd, Mead, 1904.

SAINTSBURY, GEORGE. *A Consideration of Thackeray*. London: Oxford University Press, 1931.
A reprint in book form of the Introductions to the Oxford Edition of *The Works*.

ELWIN, MALCOLM. *Thackeray: A Personality*. London: Cape, 1932.

LAS VERGNAS, RAYMOND. *Thackeray*. Paris: Champion, 1932.

ELLIS, GEOFFREY U. *Thackeray*. New York: Macmillan, 1933.

DODDS, JOHN W. *Thackeray: A Critical Portrait*. New York: Oxford University Press, 1941; Russell and Russell, 1963.

GREIG, JOHN Y. T. *Thackeray: A Reconsideration*. New York: Oxford University Press, 1950.

YOUNG, G. M. *Last Essays*. London: Hart-Davis, 1950.

FULLER, HESTER THACKERAY, AND HAMMERSLEY, V. *Thackeray's Daughter: Some Reminiscences of Anne Thackeray*. London: Euphorion, 1951.

RAY, GORDON N. *The Buried Life*. Cambridge: Harvard University Press, 1952.
A useful short study of the novels, suggesting originals for many of the characters.

TILLOTSON, GEOFFREY. *Thackeray the Novelist*. Cambridge: University Press, 1954.
A valuable study. The many quotations are well chosen to show Thackeray's quality as a stylist.

RAY, GORDON N. *Thackeray*. 2 vols. New York: McGraw-Hill, 1955–1958.
The standard biography, authorized by the Thackeray family. The first volume (*The Uses of Adversity*) carries the story up to *Vanity Fair*; the second (*The Age of Wisdom*) completes it.

CHARLES DICKENS

by K. J. Fielding

CHARLES DICKENS

Dickens in his study at Tavistock House, Bloomsbury. From a painting of 1859 by W. P. Frith in the Forster Collection of the
Victoria and Albert Museum. *Reproduced by permission of
the Victoria and Albert Museum. Crown copyright.*

CHARLES DICKENS was born on February 7, 1812, at Portsmouth. He died on June 9, 1870, at Gad's Hill, Kent, and was buried in Westminster Abbey.

CHARLES DICKENS

I. LIFE AND LETTERS

MORE BOOKS have been written about Dickens than about any other English novelist, and a distressingly large number of them have not been worth reading. Amid this mass of memoirs, biographies, introductions, critical commentaries, and miscellaneous studies, there is even more that is unreliable. Though one is planned, there is still no standard critical edition of his works; there is still no reliable edition of his letters; and, until recently, there has been no satisfactory account of his life. The great difficulty of writing about Dickens remains that hardly anything that has been written before about 1950 can be taken on trust; and yet the moment one turns back to the original sources there is the danger of being completely overwhelmed. Much of the material a biographer ought to consult, moreover, is widely dispersed or difficult of access. As a result of this, for a long while the amount of reputable criticism was small: for good criticism is written by good critics rather than 'specialists', and anyone with a reputation to lose has usually confined himself to essays and short studies rather than make the attempt to master the material for a more comprehensive commentary. In spite of Dickens's immense popularity, therefore, until quite recently he remained in many ways strangely neglected.

A general introductory essay of this length cannot hope to offer anything entirely new, and there are already sufficient general introductions. What may perhaps be of greater value is a consideration of what has been written of Dickens already, in the light of what was possible. A completely detailed survey would be impracticable; but the purpose of the present study is to examine the way in which Dickensian biography and criticism have been affected in their development by the materials that were most easily available, and this can best be illustrated by examples.

Dickens's life was dissected after his death as promptly as Dr. Johnson's: he died on 9 June 1870, and before the end of the year some half-dozen biographies had been published, none of which need be consulted now. They show only that even to his contemporaries the story of his life was almost as fascinating as his novels; that it typified much that they admired; and that they recognized that by his death they had lost a leader whose greatness was somehow representative.

They were succeeded by the standard biography of Dickens, written by his friend John Forster, which was mainly reliable and is still indispensable; for Forster had all the advantages of knowing Dickens personally, and all the disadvantages of a personal knowledge of most of his living friends and relatives. The biography suffers from certain obvious defects, the most serious of which is that the author not only omits to tell the story of Dickens's separation from his wife in anything but the vaguest outline, but leaves Mrs. Dickens out of the biography altogether. It remains a defect even though he may have had good reason for doing so. Although Dickens's affection for her appears never to have been deep, the first twenty years of their marriage seem to have been moderately happy, and even if they were not, her part in his life was not less important for that reason.

They had been married twenty-two years and she had borne him ten children. Forster himself had been accustomed to spend the anniversary of their wedding-day with them, and as his own marriage approached—only two years before their separation—he had written to Mrs. Dickens, on her birthday, to say: 'I do not know how it is that I associate you so much with the change that is about to befall me—and that I never felt so strongly as within the last few months how much of the happiness of past years I owe to you.' Nobody will blame Forster for his loyalty to Dickens, but it need not have been inconsistent with fairness to his wife; and no one else could have written of their married life with better authority. It was hardly at her wish that she was left out of the story of her husband's life.

The chief difficulty which faced Forster was the one which confronts all Dickens's biographers, and that is the enormous scope and variety of Dickens's career: every day of his life was packed with activity and incident, and almost everything he wrote cried out for quotation. Even eighty years ago there were limits to the length of a biography. Forster solved the problem in the only way he could by writing almost entirely from personal knowledge. He had been the first person to whom Dickens had confided the story of his childhood, and the only one apart from his wife; he had been consulted about everything he wrote from the publication of *Oliver Twist*; and he had acted for him in many of his personal difficulties, and all his negotiations and disputes with publishers. Although Forster had not expected to survive him, Dickens had written to his friend long before, 'I desire no better for my fame, when my personal dustiness shall be past the control of my love of order, than such a biographer and such a critic'. It is sometimes pointed out that they quarrelled outrageously on several occasions; but it remains true that Forster was the only one of Dickens's friends with whom he was ever able to differ without breaking completely. At the time he undertook his task he was, as Dickens's sister-in-law, Miss Hogarth, wrote, 'the only person with the material and the authority to write the biography'.

G. H. Lewes, echoed by Wilkie Collins, is said to have referred to his work as 'the life of Forster with notices of Dickens'. The real fault, however, is that it is not nearly personal enough. Collins made further comments in his copy of the three volume edition, which reveal nothing but his dislike for Forster. One of them was that 'The assertion (quite sincerely made) that no letters addressed by Dickens to his other old friends revealed his character so frankly and completely as his letters to Forster, it is not necessary to contradict. Dickens's letters published by his

sister-in-law and his eldest daughter may be left to settle
that question.' This edition of the *Letters* by Mary Dickens
and Georgina Hogarth settles nothing: Dickens's correspondence with Forster remains exceptional in spite of the
fact that half of it was destroyed. Collins had been consulted by Miss Hogarth about her arrangements for publication, took a great interest in the work, and gave her advice
about what she called 'the technical part' as well; but
anyone who could be satisfied with her achievement as an
editor, was no fit judge of Forster's merits or demerits as a
biographer. These criticisms by Collins were made privately
after Forster's death. He seems to have disapproved of
Forster's discretion; but although an account of his own
friendship with Dickens and their collaboration in authorship would have been invaluable, the only record he left
himself was these few jottings in a copy of another man's
biography. Comments have sometimes been made about
Forster's jealousy of Collins for supplanting him in Dickens's
friendship, and the 'mean kind of revenge' he took by
mentioning him 'no oftener than was necessary in the
biography'. But the counter-charge is equally true; and
Collins always had the remedy at hand. Instead, he saw to
it that on his death his letters from Dickens passed to Miss
Hogarth, whom he could be sure would edit them with even
greater discretion than Forster. In fact they are neither
very numerous, nor particularly valuable.

Forster's greatest sin was in destroying all the original
papers on which his work was founded. The biography
was largely composed of letters, and 'to save him time and
trouble', Mrs. Forster told Percy Fitzgerald, 'he would cut
out the passages he wanted with a pair of scissors and paste
them on his MS.'. It is impossible to verify this story since
Forster kept none of his own manuscripts once the work
was published. But even if he did mutilate most of the
letters he used it made no difference, since he made sure
that no one after him should be able to consult any but a
few of the least important. He burnt some himself, marked

others for destruction, and left instructions that it was his 'express wish that all letters coming under the denomination of private correspondence shall at once be destroyed'. The Rev. Whitwell Elwin, the editor of the *Quarterly*, who acted as his executor, held the same views as Forster about private papers, and spent several months conscientiously examining masses of correspondence and putting them aside to be burnt. Not only hundreds of Dickens's letters, but correspondence from nearly all the famous authors of the day ended thus on a bonfire at Booton Rectory.

It is no justification of Forster to say that the value set on original papers in his day was greatly different from ours: as a practised biographer, historian, and devoted collector of books and manuscripts, he was well aware of the harm he was doing. The only excuse for him is that he was probably carrying out Dickens's own instructions, since he too had burnt all the correspondence he had ever received—as far as he knew—and held strong views about an author's right to keep his private life to himself. Yet there was no need to have destroyed so much: although the manuscripts of the novels were left unharmed, important original papers such as the autobiographical fragments of Dickens's childhood and his initial outline of *The Chimes* were wantonly destroyed. In spite of Forster's generosity in leaving his library and collection of pictures and manuscripts to the Department of Science and Art, he has deprived us of even more than he bequeathed.

Forster should, perhaps, have written of Dickens simply as he knew him. 'No man's life', wrote Elwin in the *Quarterly*, 'has ever been better known to a biographer.' He had a reliable judgement, was an accomplished writer, and a sound critic. But instead of including personal reminiscences in the biography, in which he would have been unrivalled, he relied almost entirely on documents which almost anyone else might have presented equally well—and then destroyed them. His biography will always be indispensable, but it was entirely his own fault that it has now come to be regarded less as a book to be read than a work of reference.

The *Letters of Charles Dickens* (1880-2), edited by Mary Dickens and Georgina Hogarth, originated at the suggestion of the publisher, Frederick Chapman. According to the preface it was intended as 'a Supplement' to Forster's *Life*: 'That work', the editors acknowledged, 'admirable and exhaustive as a biography, is only incomplete as regards correspondence.' The letters were arranged chronologically, linked by a series of curiously uninformative 'narratives'. Editorially it conforms to contemporary standards, being heavily afflicted with major omissions and minor errors of transcription.

Yet Dickens's letters and his life will always be inseparable, and there is no doubt that this collection had an important influence on his biography for the next fifty years. Not everyone has treated it as merely supplementary to the *Life*. Forster had unquestionably been right in the emphasis he laid on the tremendous part played in Dickens's life by his works: 'Though Dickens', he wrote, 'bore outwardly so little of the impress of his writings, they formed the whole of that inner life which essentially constituted the man, and as in this respect he was actually, I have thought his biography should endeavour to present him.'

The first two editors of the *Letters*—perhaps naturally as members of the family, and inevitably in view of the desultory way in which they made their selection—concerned themselves with everything but his authorship. In publishing what they called 'the more private letters' they explained, 'we do so with the view of showing him in his homely, domestic life—of showing how in the midst of his own constant and arduous work, no household matter was considered too trivial to claim his care and attention'. Through following this course their edition left the impression of a charming eccentric who passed most of his time at the seaside with his family at Broadstairs and Boulogne, or in getting up private theatricals. Only the brilliance and vigour of the letters themselves reveal that he was also a great writer. None of them is really trivial, but the selection was uneven and the result unfortunate.

It was natural, too, that as members of the family they should have been particularly careful about including anything which might have given offence to friends of Dickens who were still alive; yet they were too preoccupied with such precutionary measures. They seem to have thought that signs of such care were expected of them even where it was unnecessary. After publication of their first two volumes, Miss Hogarth wrote to Frederick Chapman of her plans for making a third, 'I hope people who see the book will have no fear of any indiscreet use being made of their letters'. But apart from a few personal or amusing remarks about his contemporaries, there was nothing in any of his letters, even by the strictest Victorian standards, to be discreet about.

A year after the publication of the complete edition of 1882, however, a number of Dicken's letters to his solicitor, Frederic Ouvry, were published in the *New York Tribune* without the permission of his family. Some of them were copied by newspapers in this country, and Miss Hogarth (as executrix under the will) and other members of the family were naturally indignant both at such a discourtesy and the infringement of their copyright. Some of the letters contained references to the children that were harmless enough at the time they were written, but which they might understandably have preferred to have remained unpublished thirty or forty years later. The objection made by Charles Dickens, Junr., however, was not that they referred to people who were still alive, but that they re-told the story of his father's early life and the 'troubles and struggles' of his grandfather, which he thought had been treated sufficiently in Forster's *Life* and the collected *Letters*. His remarks are revealing: they show the spirit of the third generation with its growing regard for respectability. At least one of the most important reasons for the exaggerated family discretion was this sense of disgrace at Dicken's early hardships and his father's debts and irresponsibility.

In later years their apparent reluctance—for a time—to encourage further biographers was accounted for on the assumption that there was something to conceal. Recent biographers in particular, who have had no facility denied them and who have never been refused permission to print, have been quick to assume that there was good cause for what appeared to be a policy of suppression. But whatever other reasons there may also have been, their reluctance was largely due to a shamefaced desire to forget the somewhat shabby origins of the family. Some of them thought that even Forster had gone too far. Miss Hogarth and Mary Dickens had been consulted about what was to be told, but Charles Dickens, the eldest son, learnt of his father's early life for the first time when the book was published, and no doubt disapproved of it. Dicken's brother-in-law, Henry Burnett, had a deep dislike for Forster, and the same sense of the disgrace at owing money. He wrote to F. G. Kitton:

He [Forster] hated the Dickens family and said or wrote many things about them and their circumstances utterly untrue. The father of Dickens was imprudent even to a fault but never in poverty . . . . Mrs. Dickens's family were highly respectable, and she was born in Somerset House where her father had rooms. Dickens was hasty and his father vexed him often by thoughtlessly running into debt—and he had to clear him—and at such times no doubt things were said and written to his friend Forster that were coloured highly and not intended to be told or seen by others. Forster was jealous even when Dickens expressed warmth for his own relations.

In this case all that it has been possible to learn since about John Dickens only proves that Forster was right, and Burnett wrong. Mrs. Dickens's highly respectable father embezzled over five thousand pounds from the Navy Pay Office, and passed the rest of his life in exile in the Isle of

Man. All these charges of jealousy are double-edged, and Forster has been blamed for it more than enough: there is no doubt that he was as fair as any biographer can be. Privately he wrote to Frederic Ouvry, before he sat down to the *Life*: 'It revolts me, the exhibition I see made by those inheritors of the name of our old Friend! I long to have done with it. As far as I may!' Yet he was entirely discreet in everything he said of the family, and certainly wrote sympathetically of Dickens's father.

A similar unnecessary sense of discretion on the part of Miss Hogarth, and of Dickens's son, Sir Henry Fielding Dickens, was shown when his letters to Maria Beadnell were published in the United States in 1908. Once again they were printed without permission, and the refusal to allow any of the copies to be imported into England was the only answer to such an infringement of copyright. Naturally Miss Hogarth and Sir Henry were indignant, and they were entirely justified in demanding that their rights should be respected. But the letters themselves were entirely innocent and unexceptionable. In refusing at first even to read them; and then, after an agreement on publication, in insisting that several passages should be omitted, Sir Henry acted most unwisely. Eventually, he reluctantly gave his consent to their publication in full, but not before everyone had naturally assumed that there was something to conceal.

By this exaggerated concern for his reputation, Dickens's greatest admirers have laid themselves open to the repeated charge of creating a legend. Henry Burnett was typical. He wrote to F. G. Kitton of his letters from Dickens:

If I had in my keeping one with a sentence lowering to his character, neither you nor anyone would ever have seen it. But I have no single act or word in all my knowledge of him that I should desire to cover from enemy or friend.

If there was no need to shelter Dickens in this way, there was no need to be so insistent that it was unnecessary. Why should he have had enemies? But almost everybody who knew Dickens well showed this same possessiveness, the same defiance, and the same jealousy of anyone else with whom he was equally friendly.

II. REALISM AND FANTASY

For the next thirty years or more after his death there appeared a succession of personal memoirs and reminiscences which included recollections of Dickens. Many of the stories they told were incorporated in later biographies. A few of the more important of them were *Yesterdays With Authors* (1872) by James T. Fields, the American publisher; Edmund Yates's *Recollections and Experiences* (1884); *Charles Dickens As I Knew Him* (1885) by George Dolby, his Reading manager; and *My Father As I Recall Him* (1896) by Mary Dickens, his eldest daughter. There were many others that are also important, but to extend the list any further would be to run the risk of continuing it until there was no room for anything else.

A useful selection of contemporary reviews and posthumous 'tributes' was collected by F. G. Kitton in his *Dickensiana* (1886). He was also responsible for *Charles Dickens By Pen and Pencil* (1890), which contains the results of valuable original research besides reproductions of many portraits and sketches, while his *Charles Dickens, His Life, Writings, and Personality* (1902), although sound, was not otherwise remarkable. Robert Langton's *Childhood and Youth of Charles Dickens* (1883) was also important because it included new information which would otherwise have been lost.

A. W. Ward's *Dickens* (1882), should perhaps be mentioned: it is even more of an 'official' life than Forster's. Some of his remarks suggest that, like a number of other writers on Dickens, he was strongly influenced by Miss Hogarth. It seems unlikely that he read all his letters to

Mrs. Dickens, but of these he wrote authoritatively:

If he had ever loved his wife with that affection before which so-called incompatibilities of habit, temper, or disposition fade into nothingness, there is no indication of it in any of his numerous letters addressed to her.

But this correspondence was not published in full until 1935, and the answer to the question he decided so promptly is still a matter of opinion. When she knew she was dying, Mrs. Dickens had given these letters from her husband to her second daughter, Mrs. Perugini, with instructions that they should be published 'that the world may know he loved me once'; and the delay in carrying out her wishes was chiefly due to the doubt whether they really showed what she believed.[1]

Less useful than Ward but more significant is the entry in the *Dictionary of National Biography* (1888). It will always be consulted, but would hardly be worth noticing if it were not by the editor, Leslie Stephen. He should have passed it on to somebody else. It attempts to be fair, with very little success. Biographically it is a half-hearted summary of Forster; critically he has nothing better to say than 'if literary fame could safely be measured by popularity with the half-educated, Dickens must claim the highest position among English novelists'. His remarks have the same tone as those in many of the higher-class reviews written towards the end of Dickens's lifetime. It is not

---

[1] More than twenty of them were included, with minor omissions, in the collected *Letters* edited by Mary Dickens and Miss Hogarth. It is improbable that Ward formed his judgement on these alone. It has sometimes been stated that Miss Hogarth showed her jealousy of her sister by cutting out Dickens's more affectionate references to his wife (Jack Lindsay, *Charles Dickens*, 1951, p. 339). A comparison of the two texts does not support this view. Moreover, although they had disagreed at the time of the separation, the two sisters were reconciled during Mrs. Dickens's last illness. Miss Hogarth wrote of her to Ouvry: 'I really think she has taken the greatest interest and greatest pleasure in the Book . . . and . . . besides the sad circumstances, this has been a real happiness to Mamie and me.' Mrs Dickens died the same week that the *Letters* were published.

always recognized how hostile they were. The *West-minster Review* was usually disapproving, *Blackwood's* was captious, *The Times* veered from one extreme to the other, Walter Bagehot's essay in the *National Review* (1858) was perceptive but severe, and one of the most important contemporary judgements, by G. H. Lewes in the *Fortnightly* (1871), was damaging enough to call for a defence by Forster in the third volume of the *Life*. None of them, however, was so extreme as those by Leslie Stephen's elder brother, Sir James Fitzjames Stephen, who had reviewed Dickens with judicial severity and studied dislike in the pages of the *Saturday Review*. The best and most moderate critics (Lewes and Bagehot) were no doubt sincere; but remarks of some of the others, including both the Stephens, suggest that the causes for contemporary disapproval of the novels were due to class-prejudice and a dislike of his social criticism rather than purely critical considerations.

The first full-length critical study of Dickens, by George Gissing in 1898, is still one of the best. It should be read with his introductions to the unfinished Rochester edition of the novels, which were collected by B. W. Matz under the title of *The Immortal Dickens*, in 1925. They are always said to have been the work of a pessimist, although this has nothing to do with his critical remarks, but they are chiefly valuable as the appreciation of a realist. Gissing could remember, as a child, looking through the original monthly numbers of *Our Mutual Friend*, in their green paper covers; and as a young man he made himself familiar with the streets and sights of London, when 'they were simply the scenes of Dickens's novels'. In commenting on the familiar localities and characters of his fiction he spoke from knowledge: 'I believe him to have been', he wrote, 'what he always claimed to be, a very accurate painter of the human beings, no less than of the social conditions he saw about him.'

As a realist himself he appreciated the avowed purpose with which the novels were written, and called attention to the preface to the third edition of *Oliver Twist* (1841) in which Dickens had met the protest of readers who found it 'coarse and shocking', by declaring that 'as the stern and plain truth . . . was a part of the purpose of this book, I will not, for these readers, abate one hole in the Dodger's coat, or one scrap of curl-paper in the girl's dishevelled hair'. For examples and precedents Dickens looked back to the eighteenth-century novelists, but Gissing recognized his declaration as something new: 'Imagine his preface to have been written fifty years later, and it would be all but appropriate to some representative of a daring school of "naturalism", asserting his right to deal with the most painful facts of life.' In spite of Monk's theatrical rant, Oliver's gentility, and 'the feeble idyllicism of the Maylie group', he saw that Dickens's insistence that the story was 'emphatically God's truth', was a step in literary and social history: 'Think what we may of his perfectly sincere claim, the important thing, in our retrospect, is the spirit in which he made it.'

As a realist his appreciation of Dickens's pathos is particularly significant; and for the same reason his comments on the death of Paul Dombey are equally remarkable:

That the story is at this point too long drawn out everyone must admit; it was one of the unhappy results of a method of publication for which no good word could be said; but to some readers, not wholly uncritical, the child's deathbed is still genuinely pathetic, though they cannot speak of it in the terms of excited eulogy which flattered the author's ears. Paul Dombey is a picture of childhood such as only Dickens could draw; abounding in observation, enriched with imaginative sympathy; a thing very touching and tender. Remember, too, that in the forties, such a picture as this was a national benefaction; England sadly needed awakening to her responsibilities in the matter of childhood . . . . So often has the effect been aimed at by subsequent novelists that it has grown a weariness, and is too often an obvious insincerity; we are apt to forget that Dickens imitated no one, that he spoke from his heart at the prompting of his genius. The thing has perhaps been more artistically done; never with truer emotion or gentler touch.

Gissing was the first to combine purely literary criticism and general comment with an understanding of Dickens's intentions and the times in which he wrote. He does no less justice to his idealism and moral purpose, and to 'his task in life, to embody the better dreams of ordinary men'.

Chesterton's *Charles Dickens* (1906) was intended as a counterblast to Gissing. The whole book is a magnificent paradox; it professes to be no more than a mere outline, or 'personal judgement', but, slight as it is, it is too great a work to be dismissed lightly. It is undeniably more about its author than anything else, but contains nothing better than his brief sketch of Dickens in the chapter on the 'Life and Later Works'. Yet for the later novels he had little but faint praise, and advised that 'if you are in the company of any ardent adorers of Dickens, . . . do not insist too urgently and exclusively on the splendour of Dickens's last works, or they will discover that you do not like him'. As an interpretation it succeeds by the rare union of brilliance and enthusiasm.

The virtue and defect of his book is that it is chiefly 'a personal judgement'. It celebrates only the Dickens Chesterton understood best; an exuberant Dickens, an indignant Dickens, and above all a Dickens full of the Christmas spirit of charity and merry-making. He was bent on proving that Dickens was a good Chestertonian and particularly concerned to defend him as an optimist, as if anything less would have been fatal to his reputation as a serious writer. Much that he had to say was anything but literary criticism or biography. He was quite prepared to admit that Dickens had faults, but incapable of seeing any but those he was immediately prepared to absolve. He mentioned in passing Dickens's 'secret moderation', but only in alliance with what he calls 'a general wildness approaching lunacy'. He would have been too horrified at the idea even to consider that with his flamboyance in dress went a deep reserve of manner, and that he had an intense belief in respectability.

Chesterton shared with other biographers the fault of spoiling a good story by exaggeration. He described Dickens's immense achievement in the five years following *Pickwick*, as 'The Great Popularity':

> His raging and sleepless nights, his wild walks in the darkness, his note-books crowded, his nerves in rags, all this extraordinary output was but a fit sacrifice to the ordinary man. He climbed towards the lower classes. He panted upwards on weary wings to reach the heaven of the poor. . . .

Yet at this time Dickens did not go for wild night walks, he slept as well as anyone, his nerves were perfectly firm, and there were no crowded note-books—one only was started, in 1855. A few pages later Chesterton went on:

> This is the ultimately amazing thing about Dickens; the amount there is of him. He wrote, at the very least, sixteen thick books packed full of original creation. And if you could have burnt them all he could have written sixteen more, as a man writes idle letters to his friend.

Yet although it is true that he was capable of writing everyday correspondence with zest, precision, and felicity, once the first five years from 1836-41 were passed the novels were composed with laborious care and an intense concern to unite keenness of wit with directness of phrase. Dickens, moreover, became deeply disturbed at the increasingly heavy tax each successive novel laid on his imagination; and after this first success his whole life can be largely interpreted as an attempt to escape from the demands of fiction.

Chesterton recognized that 'even if we are not interested in Dickens as a great event in English literature, we must still be interested in him as a great event in English history'; but though he fully appreciated the effect of Dickens on history, he refused to write about the effect of history on Dickens. It is difficult to accept his opinion that there is no reason why the characters 'should be in one novel more

SAM WELLER AT THE SWARRY

One of the few remaining pages of the Pickwick MS. (chapter xxxvii) showing something of Dickens's liveliness and rapidity, at this time, tempered by second thoughts.

By courtesy of the Trustees of the British Museum

than another'. Dickens was peculiarly sensitive to the changing spirit of the time, to which everything he wrote conformed; and as the decades of the nineteenth century, had as strong an individual character as those of our own, all the novels and characters after the very early period are completely distinct in spirit and purpose. Although they are similar in structure, for example, the optimism of *David Copperfield* and the ironic pessimism of *Great Expectations* are sharply contrasted in both character and action; even outside the two novels, in Australia, it is impossible to imagine Magwitch the transported convict meeting Micawber the successful emigrant. Again, Will Fern, the rickburner of *The Chimes* (1844), would have been entirely out of place in the world of *Hard Times* ten years later when the struggle had been taken up by the Trade Unions. The geniality of Pickwick and the vulgarity of the Veneerings belong to different historical periods, not different personal moods.

In trying to maintain Dickens's supremacy as a creative writer Chesterton under-estimated the way in which his invention was stimulated by real people as well as by actual events and the world he lived in. In describing the 'Dickens world as a fairy-land' he concluded:

He denied his divine originality, and pretended that he had plagiarized from life. He disowned his own soul's children, and said he had picked them up in the street.

Yet even though Dickens was sometimes unwilling to admit that he had used real people as models, dozens of examples are known which show that he did. When writing *Hard Times* he even went out of his way to deny the charge of drawing from life before it was made: in a letter to his friend Peter Cunningham he objected to his having publicly stated that by 'Coketown' in the novel he meant Preston, because, he wrote, 'it will cause, as I know by former experience, characters to be fitted on to individuals whom

I never saw or heard of in my life'. Yet there is no possible doubt (although it has not been pointed out before) that the trade union organizer Slackbridge, in *Hard Times*, was drawn directly from a local strike leader, Mortimer Grimshaw, whom Dickens had both seen and heard on the visit he paid to Preston. He was described as 'Gruffshaw' in an article Dickens wrote for *Household Words* called 'On Strike'.

It may not be the least virtue of Chesterton's work that it arouses contradiction. The chief objection is not to his book, which is inimitable, but to his general method which is representative of many others: to its forceful generalizations and the assumption that an interesting personal consideration is somehow valuable even where it is wrong. His work is taken as an example and examined in more detail only because it is much better than the others, and because it has had a greater influence. Even so, if Chesterton has begun to be criticized by recent critics in his turn, it is not simply, as Sir Desmond MacCarthy supposed, that his judgement 'is no longer appreciated at its true value'. Everyone would gladly agree with him that his book is 'one of the most subtle examples of imaginative response in English criticism'; but imaginative criticism can sometimes be misleading. In this case it may be said that it deserves to be read for itself alone. Chesterton's introductions to the reprints in the Everyman's Library, which were collected as *Appreciations and Criticisms* (1911) are less exuberant, but no less perceptive.

III. MAN AND NOVELIST

For the next thirty years after Chesterton, interest in Dickens both broadened and contracted, it entered fields which had nothing to do with literature and yet became peculiarly specialized: it was a period when interest in Dickens centred almost exclusively on 'The Man' to the neglect of the novelist. Even during his lifetime the beginnings of a legend could be seen, and indeed Dickens cultivated it himself; but once he was dead it was greatly intensified. His social criticism lost its immediate force and was set aside. Popular admiration for Dickens as a great writer and an independent 'radical' was divided between the general public who accepted him passively as a great novelist suitable for children, and a narrow cult whose followers included genuine enthusiasts, vague admirers, and fanatical collectors. His 'message', which had always been imprecise, became almost anything anybody cared to make it, while attention was focused more and more sharply on his private life and personal character. Within this period there was no development in the appreciation of his work, only the accumulation of commentary and newly edited material, some of it valuable, much of it worthless and most of it independent of everything else.

It is impossible to keep to a chronological arrangement in considering the rest of the works about Dickens published in this century; they must be divided into different groups.

After 1934 the biographies will need a section to themselves; before that date there is little to be said about them. Many were no more than popular outlines—some by well-known writers—which need not be considered. *Dickens, A Portrait in Pencil* (1928) by Ralph Straus, was a good straightforward account on more or less traditional lines; while J. W. T. Ley's annotated edition of Forster's *Life* preserved the text of the 1876 edition unaltered. Ley's notes, however, are extensive enough to deserve classification as an independent contribution to Dickens's biography, and remain extremely useful though sometimes misleading. *The Man Charles Dickens* (1929) by Edward Wagenknecht, was apparently eccentric in method, but was sound, bore the mark of a keen mind and was better documented than anything that had appeared before.

One of the most important contributions to a knowledge of Dickens was a collection of his *Miscellaneous Papers* (1908) edited by B. W. Matz. It consisted of articles which Dickens had written for *Household Words*, *All the Year Round*, and the *Examiner*, many of which had not been identified as his before and which had not been previously collected. They are not only remarkable for their brilliance and power which go far beyond ordinary journalism, but are important for an understanding of the novels and of Dickens's personal principles and beliefs. Some of them are written on the same themes as the novels; others seem to run counter to them; while many are directly autobiographical. They all suggest that, although it may be possible to infer Dickens's intentions and opinions from the novels, without a sound understanding of the contemporary scene, the controversies in which he was engaged and the principles he held, they may also easily be misunderstood. As long as one infers Dickens's intentions from his apparent achievement the two will always correspond and there will be no point in comparing them; and as long as his opinions are inferred from what is said in the novels, his fiction will obviously seem to express them directly without the least complication. But the cleavage between Dickens's private opinions and the effect of the novels, or between his actual achievement and his original intention, is one of the most profoundly significant elements in Dickens's work. Both the intention and the result are equally important to a full appreciation; and only by referring to his letters and journalism is it possible to understand why he laboured so much more severely over the later novels, and the inner conflicts they engendered.

Hard Times, for example, has always been recognized as particularly important to an understanding of Dickens's opinions about the growing struggle between capital and labour; and the difficulty he had in attempting to reconcile his sympathies with both may be easily inferred from the novel. It is equally certain from much that has been written about his intentions in this instance that they may just as easily be misunderstood. Only by referring to the article he wrote for *Household Words*, entitled 'On Strike', in which he described his visit to Preston where he went looking for copy, can the kind of difficulty he had in perceiving the causes of the struggle be fully appreciated; and only by referring to descriptions of the Preston strike by other competent observers can it be seen that he did not present an accurate account of his visit in the article in *Household Words*. Finally, only from an unpublished letter to F. O. Ward—available for anyone to consult in a Manchester collection—is it evident that the reason why he was incapable of understanding what had happened at Preston was because he was already deeply prejudiced by the conduct of certain trade union leaders in a strike at Manchester two or three years before. In the novel the causes and results of the two disputes are confused. A discerning critic might infer much of this from reading *Hard Times* alone, but he could never do so without qualifying his conclusions with all kinds of modifications. It is the business of the biographer not merely to confirm critical interpretations, but to provide what Johnson called 'new certainties' on which they may both make further advances; and if they are not ready to hand the critic must provide them for himself.

Again in *Hard Times* it has always been clear that Dickens was in some way concerned about the problem of education which at the time was the centre of bitter controversy. His contemporaries expected the novel to refer to the contest which was being carried on between those who wanted state-aided schools and those who insisted that they should all be independent. But although the hard satirical style should at once have indicated to anyone familiar with Dickens's manner that it was an attack on an established institution, even the readers of his own day did not realize that Chapter II, 'The Murder of The Innocents', was intended as a satire on the activities of a Government department under the Board of Trade. The clue for this lies in the notes Dickens made as he was writing the novel, which are now with the manuscript in the Forster Collection. But although there are countless authorities on the inns and hotels visited by the Pickwickians, for years no biographer or critic even considered Dickens's notes and plans for the novels, which were obviously essential to an appreciation of his intention and method. This has now been made good by Sylvère Monod, John Butt and Kathleen Tillotson.

The soundest critics of Dickens have always recognized the importance of his interest in the contemporary scene. It was not that he was either merely a journalist or reformer, but that themes concerned with the problems of mid-nineteenth century society, its familiar scenes and people, were the chosen subject of his fiction. As popular interest in Dickens shifted from a concern with the 'message' to interest in the man, it was inevitable that attempts should be made from time to time to consider separately the social purpose of the novels. Edwin Pugh's *Charles Dickens, The Apostle of the People* (1908), was a straightforward summary of the Dickens's gospel. W. W. Crotch's *Charles Dickens, Social Reformer* (1913) was little more than an anthology of extracts which presented him simply as a humanitarian. Neither of them attempted to relate the overt subject of reform to any wider purpose in the novels, or to the way in which their themes are often expressed by Dickens's use of symbolism. The Court of Chancery in *Bleak House*, for example, is not only representative of social decay and national corruption, but was itself symbolized by the junk-shop kept by Krook, known as the 'Lord Chancellor', and his savage cat, expressive of 'strict statutes and most biting laws'. The dust heap was not introduced into *Our Mutual Friend* just because Dickens thought that similar piles of refuse, which were a common sight about London, were an insanitary nuisance. In *Little Dorrit* the financial crash of the 'house' of Merdle, which was suggested by the failure of the banker John Sadleir, is carefully related to the collapse of Mrs. Clennam's House and the ruin of the rather obviously contrived symbol of William Dorrit's 'castle in

the air'. The social purpose of the novels and their profounder meaning are almost always closely related.

The best work on Dickens's social criticism, which does
not fail to take account of all these considerations, is
Humphry House's *The Dickens World* (1941). It belongs to
the same tradition but is in an entirely different class, and is
important for a general understanding of the novels as well
as their particular relation to the contemporary scene.

It is not easy to classify T. A. Jackson's *Charles Dickens,
The Progress of a Radical* (1937). As the work of a Marxist
it is often concerned with the relation of the author to the
society in which he lived, and it is usually regarded as a
valuable commentary on the development of Dickens's
principles and beliefs. It contains some most perceptive
criticism but is constantly swerving into generalization and
detail which cannot be readily accepted. In the course of
his critical analysis Jackson came to the conclusion, in all
seriousness, that Dickens drew his characters 'in the flat'
because that is how they actually were, crushed out of shape
by the pressure of capitalist society. Thoughout his study
he was unwilling to recognize anything in Dickens's work
with which he disagreed.

The most important and reliable record of Dickens's
life, his development as an author, and his relation with
other men of the time and the society in which he lived, is
to be found in his letters. Although they are by no means
the only source for a biographer, they are the most detailed
and extensive. Dickens's letter to Maria Beadnell, the
'original' of Dora in *David Copperfield*, have already been
referred to. His correspondence with W. H. Wills, the
sub-editor of *Household Words* and *All the Year Round* was
collected in an incomplete form by R. C. Lehmann in
Charles Dickens as Editor (1912). Other collections of letters
to Henry Kolle, Mark Lemon, Miss Burdett Coutts, Thomas
Beard, Charles Lever, Mrs. Dickens and many more have
also been made; and all, except those to Mrs. Dickens, were
included in the *Letters of Charles Dickens*, edited by Walter

Dexter, in an edition of the complete works published by the Nonesuch Press in 1938.

This new edition of the letters was undoubtedly the most important work that had been published on Dickens since the biography by Forster; and the editor deserves praise for initiating it and for carrying it out. Yet it was published in a limited edition of only 877 copies, it was inaccurate, and in spite of its immense scope (4,000 letters) it was not even half complete. Nevertheless it was directly responsible for a revival of interest in Dickens's biography; and although the preparation of a new edition of the letters is now in progress it still remains indispensable. When the new edition is at last finished it will be found that Dickens's *Letters* are more than a monument to scholarship. They have a rare literary value, and more than any comparable document in our literature—from the *Paston Letters* to Pepys' *Diary* or Boswell's *Journals*—they will bring us vitally into contact with an extraordinary man, with the feel of every day, with the creation of his work, with his great and influential public career and the astonishing variety of his life.

IV. REVELATIONS AND INTERPRETATIONS

Meanwhile, a new departure in Dickens's biography began with the publication of an article in the *Daily Express* of 3 April 1934, by Thomas Wright. It was entitled '98 Years Ago To-day—Charles Dickens Began His Honeymoon'; but it had nothing to do with the beginning of his marriage, only with its failure, his separation from his wife and what is said to have followed. The importance of this article lay entirely in the repetition of a story which had been told to Wright, nearly forty years before, by one of his friends, Canon William Benham. For although it had always been known that the name of a young actress, Miss Ellen Lawless Ternan, had been linked with Dickens's in the gossip which followed his break with his wife, none of his biographers had ever questioned before that Dickens's public denial of this scandal was entirely genuine. Even now Wright accepted that Dickens's declaration was perfectly true at the time it was made—immediately following the separation—but, after a long preamble, he went on to introduce his story with the outright assertion that, 'I can state positively, my authority being Canon Benham, that Miss Ternan did later become Dickens's mistress'.

As the story goes, Dickens first met Miss Ternan in the green-room of one of the leading London theatres. It is said to have been 'her first appearance as an actress, and she was weeping bitterly because she had to appear in very scanty attire'; Dickens reassured her, and thus their friendship began. When three professional actresses were needed for a performance of Dickens's company of amateur players, to be given at Manchester in August 1857, she was engaged with her mother and elder sister. In the months that followed, Dickens had always been known to have grown more and more restless, until he finally broke free in May 1858. According to Canon Benham, the immediate cause of this separation was the unfortunate mis-delivery to Mrs. Dickens of a bracelet which Dickens had bought as a present for Miss Ternan. There was nothing else to be added to the story of the separation as it had been known before, but some time after this, according to Wright, 'Miss Ternan became Dickens's mistress':

> Then followed all the trouble. It spoilt her life, for although the close intimacy could not have lasted long she was tortured by remorse, and later she took her trouble to Canon Benham, who had become her spiritual adviser. She told him the whole story and declared she loathed the very thought of this intimacy.

Stripped of Wright's comments this was the whole story; and in this form, before he and other biographers began to confuse it with their conjectures, it called for the most serious consideration. Naturally there were doubts about whether it was true; but no one can question its direct influence on almost all of Dickens's later biographers and critics.

The most obvious point about the way in which Wright treated the story was that Benham was never an 'authority' for the original facts; his importance lay solely in being one of the links between Miss Ternan and the present day. Wright could vouch for nothing more than the story as it had been told to him by his friend, for everyone else whom it concerned was dead. The only question that remained was whether Wright, Canon Benham or Miss Ternan could have been either mistaken or deliberately misleading in the account which they passed from one to another? Judging by its subsequent career this was the kind of tale that develops rapidly once it has been started, and might well have been altered completely in its transition from the vicar's study in Margate to the centre-page of the *Daily Express*. Yet there are now good reasons for believing that Wright acted in entire good faith. It seems certain that, some time during the sixties, Ellen Ternan became Dickens's mistress; but whether Canon Benham reported her rightly, and just what their personal relations were, it is still impossible to say.

The following year was published Wright's *Life of Charles Dickens*. It is still a useful book to anyone who is already well informed about Dickens, but it was not well written, the new material was badly presented, and it was frequently inaccurate. As a result of the controversy it caused, however, further details about Dickens's later association with Miss Ternan were brought to Wright's notice which he published in his *Autobiography* in 1936. Briefly, he learnt that according to local gossip in Camberwell, Dickens was said to have been a frequent visitor of a lady at Windsor Lodge, 16 Linden Grove, between 1867 and 1870; he was told that her name was 'Miss Turnham'; that she was said to have been a relative of Trollope; that Dickens used the alias of 'Charles Tringham'; and that she was said to have been 'his unofficial wife'. He knew that Miss Ternan's sister Frances had married Thomas Adolphus Trollope in 1866; and, on inquiry, he found out that the names of Turnham and Tringham were confirmed by entries in the local rate-books, which also showed that the rates were paid by one or other of them from July 1867 to July 1870. If it is assumed that Ternan and Turnham were the same, the dates fit exactly. She is known to have left another address in 1867 and to have gone abroad soon after Dickens's death in June 1870. The supposition that Wright found the 'corroborative' details first and then made up the story to fit them is entirely untenable: if necessary it could be shown to be false.

Further confirmation was added on the publication of Miss Gladys Storey's *Dickens and Daughter*, in 1939. Miss Storey had been a close friend of Mrs. Perugini, who was Dickens's second daughter, Kate. She had died in 1929, but some time during her last illness she had told Miss Storey what she knew of the causes of the separation of her father and mother, which she asked her to make known after her death. Although it contained many additional details her account was not very different from Canon Benham's; indeed, she should obviously have been more careful to distinguish between the two versions. It is impossible, however, to question her good faith, and the general truth of her account cannot be rejected unless it is supposed that Mrs. Perugini was too old and ill to know what she was saying. There is evidence that this was not so; and it is also known that Miss Storey was not the only friend in whom she confided, although she alone was left with the task of publishing the story as it had been told to her.

All this left everyone dissatisfied. It was not simply a matter of pandering to posterity's inquisitiveness. Dickens, himself, at the time of his separation from his wife, had been the first to recognize that his private affairs were bound to concern his public. He had set himself up as a moralist; he had sung the praises of family life and the home; and he had placed a special value on the sincerity of his relations with his readers. If it were to be shown, then, that his life belied his teaching, it might well have various consequences. At its very simplest, it might appear to justify the belief that his books were more superficial, and his life more complicated, than had generally been supposed.

Yet, in itself, it may well be thought that the importance of the affair has been both over-stressed and over-simplified. Dickens did not meet Miss Ternan until some time in 1857, so that for the first forty-five years of his life, in which he wrote the greatest part of his work, she could have had no influence on him. There is no doubt that their friendship was the immediate cause of the separation, but his marriage was already a failure. The many details that have more recently been discovered about their association after 1858, still leave us knowing almost as little of real interest about it as of the relations between Shakespeare and Anne Hathaway.

It is necessary to insist on this because several biographers have tried to fill in these outlines by using their imagination. Few of them followed up Wright's investigations. Instead they have adopted the alternative course of trying to fill in the details of the story of Dickens's association with Miss Ternan by identifying them both with the chief characters of the later novels.

The only justification of this method is that, rather more than most other novelists, Dickens is recognized to have used incidents from his own experience in writing fiction, and once it is known where he did so it is usually easy to see how they correspond. On the other hand, apart from some of the autobiographical passages in *David Copperfield*, it is difficult to recall a single instance in which a critic has successfully been able to use his knowledge of the novels to infer what actually happened in real life. Apart from the more obvious limitations of this method it is entirely useless (except as a means of giving more latitude to the merely 'personal judgment'), since there was always a time-lag before Dickens drew on his actual experiences for fiction, and except for the intensity with which he wrote it is impossible to say that he identified himself with one character more than another. Finally, wherever we are able to recognize that he did rely on experience it is evident that he did so quite consciously, while all such interpretations depend on the belief that his passion for Miss Ternan (or his disappointment that his love was not returned) was expressed subconsciously in the novels. It is never explained precisely how or why Dickens identified himself with some of the characters: whether he did so directly or indirectly, whether they expressed his hopes or his fears, his experience or his frustration. However valuable a psychological interpretation may be in interpreting what we know of the first twelve years of his life, it may easily confuse our understanding of what we do not know of the last.

V. RECENT BIOGRAPHY

These biographers were Hugh Kingsmill, *The Sentimental Journey* (1934), Dame Una Pope-Hennessy, *Charles Dickens, 1812–1870* (1945), Hesketh Pearson, *Dickens, His Character, Comedy and Career* (1949), Jack Lindsay, *Charles Dickens, A Biographical and Critical Study* (1950), and Julian Symons, *Charles Dickens* (1951). All of them have used much the same methods, and almost all have been strongly influenced by the story of Dickens's association with Ellen Ternan. Something, however, should be said to distinguish them.

Hugh Kingsmill made much of Wright's new discoveries, for he promptly decided that although Miss Ternan at first appealed to Dickens's idealism, 'she soon became the object of his sensuality with which he tried to drug the unhappiness of his later years'. Apart from the Ternan affair the whole biography suffers from the method of coming to conclusions first and finding reasons afterwards. In the final chapter, for example, in order to support his contention that Dickens preferred Wilkie Collins's friendship and was contemptuous of Forster as early as 1858, he inferred that a remark about 'solemn imposters' in one of Dickens's letters to Collins was intended to apply to Forster because of his opposition to the public readings; yet a brief investigation would have shown that it referred to members of the committee of a literary society with whom Dickens, supported by Forster, was engaged in controversy. A few pages later, in order to substantiate his assertion that Dickens showed an obvious 'mental and moral deterioration' after about 1867, he cited an incident which he supposed to have taken place in 1868 but which his source clearly shows to have happened some time in the 'forties. Such mistakes matter mainly in principle: they are chiefly important because they show a misunderstanding of Dickens's character. In 1858 he could not have written in such a way, and in 1868 he could never have behaved as he did twenty or thirty years before.

The Nonesuch edition of the *Letters* led to a revival of interest in Dickens's biography, and Dame Una Pope-Hennessy acknowledged that her book was 'for the most part based' upon it. Her account fulfilled the need for a popular narrative of the events of his life. Hesketh Pearson's biography was of a similar kind, written in a lively manner; it was keenly critical and sometimes probably unjust, but it gave a brisk and accurate account within the limits he set himself of reliance on published work alone. Both were accounts of Dickens's life rather than studies of his work.

Jack Lindsay's biography was an attempt to consider both the man and the author; but it is more valuable as a critical study than an outline of the life. As a psychological interpretation it is often highly questionable; it is frequently inaccurate; and although it was written in a critical spirit it shows little discrimination between various authorities. Yet it was the first full-length critical study of Dickens after Gissing and Chesterton, and is particularly valuable for its examination of Dickens's fantasy, his creative impulses, and the themes and symbols into which they forced themselves in spite of both the tension of his own inner conflicts and his outward revolt against the values of the age. Jack Lindsay's attempt 'to relate Dickens's work to the processes of history' is always interesting and often helpful to an understanding of the novels. Everything he has to say of the influence of Sir Edward Bulwer-Lytton is extremely important. But he probably exaggerates Dickens's understanding of his own times.

In emphasizing the influence of the affair with Ellen Ternan on the novels, like most of the recent biographers, he fails to show where it lies. It may well be that it had some effect, but it is unlikely to have been important. Dickens had long before given up his allegiance to most Victorian conventions, so that it is extremely doubtful whether it affected his views on society; while although he may have shown a greater understanding of women in the later novels (in Bella Wilfer, Lizzie Hexam, and Helena Landless) they were still only of minor interest. What remains to be understood is how extraordinary it was that Dickens should have led such a double life; how strangely he was immersed in the world of his day and yet kept himself apart; and how that old 'unhappy want of something' he had felt since the *Copperfield* days was to be satisfied neither by reform, companionship, or the cult of his own personality In his last decade he was more complex as a man and a writer than has usually been allowed.

Incomparably the best brief critical studies of Dickens are two essays, one by George Orwell in *Inside the Whale* (1940), reprinted in *Critical Essays* (1946), and the other by Edmund Wilson, 'Dickens: The Two Scrooges', in *The Wound and the Bow* (1941). To Orwell, Dickens was remarkable as a progressive without interest in the future, a social rebel who was really a moralist and an English radical who was a national institution. The value of his essay depends on a genuine understanding of Dickens based on sympathy and knowledge without any pretence to peculiar powers of critical divination denied to everyone else. He recognized that Dickens 'was *not*, as Messrs. Chesterton and Jackson seem to imply, a "proletarian" writer', and found that he represented in a memorable form 'the native decency of the common man';

> From the Marxist or Fascist point of view, nearly all that Dickens stands for can be written off as 'bourgeois morality'. But in moral outlook no one could be more 'bourgeois' than the English working classes. . . . All through the Christian ages, and especially since the French Revolution, the Western world has been haunted by the idea of freedom and equality; it is only an *idea*, but it has penetrated to all ranks of society. . . . Nearly everyone, whatever his actual conduct may be, responds emotionally to the idea of human brotherhood. Dickens voiced a code which was and on the whole still is believed in, even by people who violate it.

Edmund Wilson's essay, 'Dickens: The Two Scrooges', purports to be about the psychological interest of Dickens's life and works: the title refers to his 'dualism', the division of everything into good and bad: in fact, it is much more important for its analysis of Dickens's isolated position in society, caught between two classes—'an excellent thing for a novelist from the point of view of his art, because it enables him to dramatize contrasts and to study relations which the dweller in one world cannot know'. Dickens is shown to have begun by insisting that the highest and lowest elements in society were inextricably linked together in spite of 'the English hierarchical system', and to have demonstrated in his own work that morality and social criticism were likewise inseparable:

> Dickens had at first imagined that he was pillorying abstract faults in the manner of the comedy of humours: Selfishness in *Chuzzlewit*, Pride in *Dombey*. But the truth was that he had already begun an indictment against a specific society: the self-important and moralizing middle-class who had been making such rapid progress in England and coming down like a damper on the bright fires of English life. . . .

As a biographical interpretation it makes a plot out of the raw materials of the life, but it omits too much to be entirely convincing. As a critical consideration it is difficult to follow without being certain in what sense the author supposes Dickens identified himself with the criminal and rebel. His analysis of the dualism in Dickens's nature has not been carried sufficiently far. If 'Dickens' is simply the term for an abstraction from the major novels his explanation is admittedly a masterly summary; but in so far as it also stands for the man who had a great public career apart from his work as a novelist, and whose strongly pronounced personal opinions on all the social questions of the day were openly expressed in his letters, public speeches and works of journalism as well as his fiction, then many of his generalizations remain unacceptable.

In arguing that Dickens 'identified himself readily with the thief, and even more readily with the murderer', Mr. Wilson makes a point of mentioning that he 'wrote letters to the press in protest against capital punishment for murderers'; but he does not explain that this opinion was later modified, and that Dickens was himself attacked by all-out abolitionists for being what they called a supporter of 'secret hangings', while his old friend Douglas Jerrold quarrelled with him because he confined his opposition to *public* executions. As Orwell noticed, moreover, the chapter at the end of *David Copperfield* in which David visits the prison in which Littimer and Uriah Heep are serving their sentences, shows that he regarded such 'model' prisons as too humane. The man who identified himself with the criminal was anxious at one time to become a magistrate and was an admirer of the police. He was undoubtedly fascinated by the psychology of murderers, but he was repelled as well as attracted and strongly attacked the morbid interest that was taken in their trials by the public. He was for reducing legal safeguards in favour of the stricter and more efficient execution of justice. In later life Dickens was no more a mere humanitarian then Carlyle.

Mr. Wilson has made a brilliant critical examination of the novels, and has given in his theory of dualism a tempting method of analysing Dickens himself. It would, however, be misleading to apply this theory of dualism too literally, and to conclude that Dicken's characters were organized simply according to a division between good and bad sentimentality and severity, generosity and shrewdness.

Although it is undoubtedly true that Dickens expressed much in the novels to which he would have been unwilling to commit himself in any other form, it was a mistake to read them as if they were nothing more than a dreamlike projection of his subconscious fears and desires. The more closely they are studied the clearer it is that the most consciously contrived elements in his work—often the least typically 'Dickensian'—are not the least important.

For as long as his opinions and life were mainly inferred from his novels, there was only a lifeless or uncertain correspondence between them. But now, as the facts of his life have largely been stabilized and criticism has become more responsible, there has begun to be the necessary tension between them for one to respond to the other. The publication of Edgar Johnson's biography of Dickens (1953) marked a great step forward. The later works that have been added to the 'select bibliography' (pp. 130-140) show how much greater attention has recently been paid to Dicken's skill and craftsmanship as a novelist.

Other studies have carried us further and introduced us to Dickens as an artist whose novels show us a conception of life far more personal and profound than, until recently, even his greatest admirers believed in. A debate remains to be carried on between those who wish to pursue these analyses and those who are turning to a study of his language. Further advances may be expected here; for Dickens's stylistic lapses were so obvious and are still so little to our liking that less has been written of his mastery of expression than almost any other aspect. Yet much of his art and the pleasure he gives lay on the surface: in his dialogue, in the manipulation of his characters, and in the assured and flexible tones of a writer whose triumph in presenting his novels (and himself through his novels) was quite as much one of art and style as of character.

For many years, almost all criticism of Dickens might be seen as an attempt to answer the misgivings of G. H. Lewes that in spite of their power 'thought is strangely absent from his works'. Lewes was at a loss to account for their success. At various times the explanation has been found in Dickens's goodwill, the penetration of his analysis and criticism of society, his humour and high spirits, his sheer skill, or his use of symbols to shadow forth his own obsessions or the dilemmas of the human condition. It is now being seen that there is no simple answer: his success rests on all these things, and in the complexity of his imaginative realization of life and in the vitality of his language.

'If you wish to preserve the spirit of a dead author', wrote Samuel Butler, 'you must not skin him, stuff him, and set him up in a case. You must eat him, digest him, and let him live in you, with such life as you have, for better or worse.' Dickens still resists the taxidermist. Perhaps more than any other writer of the last century he remains, in this sense, a living author.

CHARLES DICKENS

Select Bibliography

BIBLIOGRAPHIES

SHEPHERD, RICHARD H. *The Bibliography of Dickens: A bibliographical list arranged in chronological order of the published writings in prose and verse (from 1834 to 1880)*. Manchester, 1880.

KITTON, F. G. *Dickensiana: A bibliography of the literature relating to Charles Dickens and his writings*. London: Redway, 1886.

KITTON, F. G. *The Minor Writings of Charles Dickens: A bibliography and sketch*. London: Stock, 1886.

ECKEL, J. C. *The First Editions of the Writings of Charles Dickens and Their Values: A Bibliography*. New York: Inman, 1932.
First edition 1903: the later edition is much revised and enlarged. Mainly for collectors.

Charles Dickens: An excerpt from the general catalogue of printed books in the British Museum. London: The British Museum, 1926.

HATTON, T., AND CLEAVER, A. H. *A Bibliography of the Periodical Works of Charles Dickens: Bibliographical, analytical, and statistical*. London: Chapman and Hall, 1933.
Mainly for collectors.

MILLER, WILLIAM. *The Dickens Student and Collector: A list of writings relating to Charles Dickens and his works, 1836–1945*. Cambridge: Harvard University Press, 1946.

Note. Most of the MSS of the novels are in the Forster Collection at the Victoria and Albert Museum, London. There are other major MSS collections in the Pierpont Morgan Library, New York, and the Henry E. Huntington Library, San Marino, California.

COLLECTED EDITIONS

Works. 17 vols. London: Chapman and Hall, 1847–1868.
The "first cheap edition."

Library Edition. 22 vols. London: Chapman and Hall, 1858–1859.
This was reissued in 30 vols., 1861–1874, with new title pages.

The Charles Dickens Edition. 21 vols. London: Chapman and Hall, 1867–1874.

The Works. With Introductions by Charles Dickens the younger. 20 vols. London: Macmillan, 1892–1925.

Gadshill Edition. Edited by Andrew Lang. 36 vols. New York: Scribner's, 1897–1908. Including Dickens's *Miscellaneous Papers*, Vols. XXXV and XXXVI edited by B. W. Matz (1908) which mainly comprises his articles in *Household Words* and *All the Year Round* not collected in *Reprinted Pieces* and *Uncommercial Traveller*, and others contributed to the *Examiner*, *Daily News*, *Cornhill*, etc. The *Miscellaneous Papers* were included in the National and Centenary Editions (1908 and 1911) and in the Nonesuch Edition (1938) under the title of *Collected Papers*. They have also been reprinted separately.

Authentic Edition. 21 vols. New York: Scribner's, 1901–1906.

Oxford India Paper Dickens. 17 vols. New York: Oxford University Press, 1901–1902.

Biographical Edition. Edited by A. Waugh. 20 vols. London: Chapman and Hall, 1902–1903.

National Edition. 40 vols. London: Chapman and Hall, 1906–1908.

Centenary Edition. 36 vols. New York: Scribner's, 1910–1911.

The Waverley Edition. 30 vols. London: Waverley, 1913–1915.
With introductions by well-known authors, including one by G. B. Shaw on *Hard Times*.

The Nonesuch Dickens. Edited by A. Waugh, W. Dexter, T. Hatton, and H. Walpole. 23 vols. Bloomsbury: Nonesuch, 1937–1938.

New Oxford Illustrated Dickens. 21 vols. New York: Oxford University Press, 1947–1959.

Oxford Dickens. General editors, John Butt and Kathleen Tillotson. A new edition of Dickens's works, planned to present a revised text which takes into account original manuscripts, proofs, and author's revisions. The first two volumes to appear will probably be *Oliver Twist* and *David Copperfield*.

LETTERS

HOGARTH, GEORGINA, AND DICKENS, MARY (eds.). *The Letters of Charles Dickens. Edited by his Sister-in-law and Eldest Daughter*. 3 vols. London: Chapman and Hall, 1880–1882.

Mr. and Mrs. Charles Dickens: His Letters to Her. Edited by W. Dexter. London: Constable, 1935.
Not included in the Nonesuch Edition, 1938.

Letters of Charles Dickens. The Nonesuch Edition. 3 vols. Edited by W. Dexter. Bloomsbury: Nonesuch, 1938.
The best and fullest edition published so far.

Letters from Charles Dickens to Angela Burdett-Coutts, 1841–62. Edited by E. Johnson. London: Cape, 1953; Boston: Little, Brown, 1952.
The American edition is entitled *The Heart of Charles Dickens*.

"New Letters of Charles Dickens to John Forster." Edited by G. G. Grubb and K. J. Fielding. *Boston University Studies in English*. Vol. II (1956).

The Letters of Charles Dickens. Vol. 1. 1820–1839. Edited by M. House and G. Storey. Oxford: Clarendon Press, 1965.
The first volume of what will be, when completed, the standard edition.

SPEECHES

The Speeches of Charles Dickens. Edited by K. J. Fielding. Oxford: Clarendon Press, 1960.
The definitive text; much more accurate and complete than earlier collections.

SEPARATE WORKS

Dates of first London editions are given, and modern editions and current paperbacks are also recorded here.

Sunday Under Three Heads: As it is; as Sabbath Bills would make it; as it might be made, 1836. *Essay*.
Published under the pseudonym "Timothy Sparks."

Sketches by "Boz": Illustrative of every-day life, and every-day people. 2 vols. 1836. *Essays*.
A second series in one volume appeared at the end of 1836, and the whole series in one volume, 1839.

The Village Coquettes: A Comic Opera, 1836. *Libretto*.

The Posthumous Papers of the Pickwick Club: Containing a faithful record of the perambulations, perils, travels, adventures, and sporting transactions of the corresponding members. Edited by "Boz," 1827. *Novel*.
All Dickens's novels published in monthly numbers between 1836 and 1866 appeared in twenty parts of 32 pages; numbers XIX and

XX, however, were always issued together as a so-called "double number" of only 48 pages. *Pickwick* was published from April 1836 to November 1837.
Everyman's Library; Nelson Classics; Modern Library.

The Strange Gentleman: A Comic Burletta, in two acts, 1837. *Drama.*
Based on "The Great Winglebury Duel" in *Sketches by "Boz."*

Is She His Wife? Or Something Singular: A Comic Burletta in one act, 1837. *Drama.*

Sketches of Young Gentlemen: dedicated to the young ladies, 1838. *Essays.*
Published anonymously.

Oliver Twist: Or, the parish boy's progress. 3 vols. 1838. *Novel.*
First published in *Bentley's Miscellany* as a monthly serial between February 1837 and March 1839. Edited by J. H. Miller (Rinehart Editions); Nelson Classics; The World's Classics; Dolphin Paperback; Everyman's Library.

The Life and Adventures of Nicholas Nickleby. Containing a faithful account of the fortunes, misfortunes, uprisings, down-fallings, and complete career of the Nickleby family, 1839. *Novel.*
First issued in twenty (as nineteen) monthly parts from April 1838. Everyman's Library; Nelson Classics.

Sketches of Young Couples: With an urgent remonstrance to the gentlemen of England (being bachelors or widowers), on the present alarming crisis, 1840. *Essays.*
Published anonymously.

Master Humphrey's Clock. 3 vols. 1840–1841. *Novels, sketches, and short stories.*
Originally issued in eighty-eight weekly parts, and also in monthly numbers, from April 4, 1840.

The Old Curiosity Shop, 1841.
In the *Clock* from April 25, 1840.
Dolphin Paperback; Everyman's Library; Nelson Classics.

Barnaby Rudge: A tale of the riots of 'eighty, 1841. *Novel.*
In the *Clock* from February 13, 1841.

American Notes, for general circulation. 2 vols. 1842. *Travel.*
Premier Paperback.

The Life and Adventures of Martin Chuzzlewit: His relatives, friends, and enemies. Comprising all his wiles and his ways, with an historical record of what he did, and what he didn't; showing, moreover, who inherited the family plate, who came in for the silver spoons, and who for the wooden ladles. The whole forming a complete key to the house of Chuzzlewit, 1844. *Novel.*

First issued in twenty (as nineteen) monthly parts from January 1843. Everyman's Library; Nelson Classics.

A Christmas Carol: In prose. Being a ghost story of Christmas, 1843. *Short story.*

The first of the Christmas books.
Dolphin Paperbacks.

The Chimes: A goblin story of some bells that rang an old year out and a new year in, 1844. *Short Story.*

The Cricket on the Hearth: A fairy tale of home, 1845. *Short Story.*

The Battle of Life: A love story, 1846. *Short Story.*

Pictures from Italy, 1846. *Travel.*

First published in the *Daily News* between January 21 and March 2, 1846, with some variations, as seven "Travelling Letters."

Dealings with the Firm of Dombey and Son, Wholesale, Retail, and for Exportation, 1848. *Novel.*

First issued in twenty (as nineteen) monthly parts from October 1846. Everyman's Library; Nelson Classics.

The Haunted Man and the Ghost's Bargain: A fancy for Christmas time, 1848. *Short Story.*

The Personal History, Adventures, Experiences, and Observations of David Copperfield the Younger of Blunderstone Rookery (Which he never meant to be published on any account), 1850. *Novel.*

First issued in twenty (as nineteen) monthly parts from May 1849. Everyman's Library; Modern Library; edited by G. Ford (Riverside Paperback).

Christmas Stories, 1850–1867. *Short Stories.*

Published as part of the Christmas numbers of *Household Words* and *All the Year Round* between 1850 and 1867, usually written either in collaboration with Wilkie Collins or in conjunction with other regular contributors.
Everyman's Library.

A Child's History of England. 3 vols. 1852–1854. *History.*

First published in *Household Words* between January 25, 1851, and December 10, 1853.

Bleak House, 1853. *Novel*.

First issued in twenty (as nineteen) monthly parts, from March 1852. Everyman's Library; Nelson Classics; edited by M. Zabel (Riverside Paperback).

Hard Times: For these times, 1854. *Novel*.

First published in *Household Words* in weekly installments from April 1 to August 12.

Everyman's Library; edited by W. W. Watt (Rinehart Editions).

Little Dorrit, 1857. *Novel*.

First issued in twenty (as nineteen) monthly parts from December 1855. Everyman's Library; Nelson Classics.

The Lazy Tour of Two Idle Apprentices, 1857. *Travel*.

In collaboration with Wilkie Collins. First published in *Household Words*, October 3 to October 31, 1857.

Reprinted Pieces, 1858. *Essays*.

First appeared in book form as part of Vol. 8 of the Library Edition of the collected works. Consists of thirty-one articles contributed to *Household Words*.

A Tale of Two Cities, 1859. *Novel*.

First published in *All the Year Round* in weekly installments from April 30 to November 26.

The World's Classics; Everyman's Library; Modern Library.

Hunted Down, 1859. *Short Story*.

First published in the *New York Ledger* of August 20, 27, and September 3, 1859; also in *All the Year Round*, August 4, 11, 1860.

Great Expectations. 3 vols. 1861. *Novel*.

First published in *All the Year Round* in weekly installments from December 1, 1860, to August 3, 1861.

Edited by Louis Crompton (The Library of Literature—Bobbs-Merrill); The World's Classics; Everyman's Library.

The Uncommercial Traveller, 1861. *Essays*.

A series of essays from *All the Year Round*; the first edition, 1861, included seventeen papers; the next, 1868, had an additional eleven; a further eight were added to the volume in an Illustrated Library Edition, 1875; and one more, making thirty-seven altogether, to the Gadshill Edition, 1908.

Our Mutual Friend. 2 vols. 1865. *Novel*.

First issued in twenty (as nineteen) monthly parts from May 1864. Everyman's Library; Nelson Classics.

George Silverman's Explanation, 1868. *Short Story*.

First published in the *Atlantic Monthly*, Boston, January to March 1868, also in *All the Year Round*, February 1, 15, 29, 1868.

Holiday Romance, 1868. *Children's Story*.

First published in *Our Young Folks*, Boston, between January and May 1868; also in *All the Year Round* between January 25 and April 4, 1868.

The Mystery of Edwin Drood, 1870. *Novel*.

Unfinished at Dickens's death. First issued in six monthly parts from April to September 1870, and originally designed to be completed in twelve.

Dolphin Paperback.

The Lamplighter: A Farce by Charles Dickens, 1838. Now first printed from a manuscript in the Forster collection at the South Kensington Museum, 1879. *Drama*.

The Life of Our Lord: Written for his children. New York: Simon and Schuster, 1934. *Religion*.

Not designed for publication.

Note. After reporting for *The Mirror of Parliament* and the *True Sun*, Dickens was engaged on the *Morning Chronicle* from August 1834 to November 1836. He edited *Bentley's Miscellany* from January 1837 to February 1839; the *Daily News* from January 21 to February 9, 1846; *Household Words* from March 1850 to May 1859; and *All the Year Round* from April 1859 until his death.

BIOGRAPHICAL AND CRITICAL STUDIES

LEWES, G. H. "Dickens in Relation to Criticism," *Fortnightly Review* (February 1872).

FORSTER, J. *The Life of Charles Dickens*. 3 vols. London: Chapman and Hall, 1872–1874; revised edition, 1876.

The most useful edition is by J. W. T. Ley in one volume (New York: Doubleday, Doran, 1928) which contains much additional material.

WARD, A. W. *Dickens*. London: Macmillan, 1882.

LANGTON, R. *The Childhood and Youth of Charles Dickens*. London: Hutchinson, 1891.

Earlier and slighter edition, 1883.

DOLBY, G. *Charles Dickens as I Knew Him: The story of his reading tours in Great Britain and America (1866–1870)*. London: Unwin, 1885.

DICKENS, MARY. *Charles Dickens: By his eldest daughter*. London: Cassell, 1885.

Reworded as *My Father as I Recall Him* (London: Roxburghe, 1896).

KITTON, F. G. *Charles Dickens by Pen and Pencil. With Supplement*. London: Sabin, 1890.

GISSING, GEORGE. *Charles Dickens: A critical study*. New York: Dodd, Mead, 1898.

KITTON, F. G. *Charles Dickens: His life, writings and personality*. London: Jack, 1902.

CHESTERTON, G. K. *Charles Dickens*. New York: Dodd, Mead, 1906.

PUGH, E. *Charles Dickens: The Apostle of the People*. London: New Age Press, 1908.

FITZGERALD, S. J. A. *Dickens and the Drama*. New York: Scribner's, 1910.

CHESTERTON, G. K. *Appreciations and Criticisms of the Works of Charles Dickens*. New York: Dutton, 1911.

PUGH, E. *The Charles Dickens Originals*. New York: Scribner's, 1912.

CROTCH, W. W. *Charles Dickens: Social Reformer*. London: Chapman and Hall, 1913.

FITZGERALD, P. H. *Memoirs of Charles Dickens*. Bristol: Arrowsmith, 1913.

SWINBURNE, A. C. *Charles Dickens*. London: Chatto and Windus, 1913.

LEY, J. W. T. *The Dickens Circle: A narrative of the novelist's friendships*. London: Chapman and Hall, 1918.

GISSING, GEORGE. *The Immortal Dickens. Introductions to the unfinished Rochester edition*. London: Palmer, 1925.

CARLTON, W. J. *Charles Dickens: Shorthand Writer*. London: Palmer, 1926. Dickens as a reporter.

DICKENS, SIR H. F. *Memories of My Father*. London: Gollancz, 1928.

STRAUS, RALPH. *Dickens: A portrait in pencil*. London: Gollancz, 1928. Reprinted as *A Portrait of Dickens* (London: Dent, 1938).

HOLDSWORTH, SIR WILLIAM S. *Charles Dickens as a Legal Historian*. New Haven: Yale University Press, 1928.

WAGENKNECHT, E. *The Man Charles Dickens: A Victorian Portrait*. Boston and New York: Houghton Mifflin, 1929.

SITWELL, OSBERT. *Dickens*. London: Chatto and Windus, 1932.

DARWIN, BERNARD. *Dickens*. London: Duckworth, 1933.

LEACOCK, STEPHEN. *Charles Dickens, his life and work*. London: Davies, 1933.

DENT, H. C. *The Life and Characters of Charles Dickens*. London: Wheeler, 1933.

MAUROIS, ANDRÉ. *Dickens*. Trans. H. Miles. London: Lane, 1934.

KINGSMILL, HUGH. *The Sentimental Journey: A life of Charles Dickens*. New York: Morrow, 1934.
Hugh Kingsmill is a pseudonym for H. K. Lunn.

WRIGHT, THOMAS. *The Life of Charles Dickens*. London: Jenkins, 1935.
———. *An Autobiography*. London: Jenkins, 1936.
Chapter XIV, subtitled "A Startling Story. New Discoveries Respecting Charles Dickens, Respecting his Life at Nunhead. . . ."

JACKSON, T. A. *Charles Dickens: The progress of a radical*. London: Lawrence and Wishart, 1937.

STOREY, G. *Dickens and Daughter*. London: Muller, 1939.

GUMMER, E. N. *Dickens' Works in Germany, 1837–1937*. Oxford: Clarendon Press, 1940.

ORWELL, GEORGE. *Inside the Whale and Other Essays*. London: Gollancz, 1940.
Includes "Charles Dickens," reprinted in *Dickens, Dali and Others* (New York: Reynal, 1946). Essential.

WILSON, EDMUND. *The Wound and the Bow: Seven studies in literature*. Boston: Houghton Mifflin, 1941.
Includes "Dickens: The Two Scrooges." Still essential.

HOUSE, HUMPHRY. *The Dickens World*. New York: Oxford University Press, 1941; 2nd ed., 1960.
An important assessment.

POPE-HENNESSY, U. *Charles Dickens, 1812–70*. London: Chatto and Windus, 1945.

SHAW, GEORGE BERNARD. "Introduction" to *Great Expectations*. The Novel Library. London: Hamilton, 1947.
Shaw's criticism is always stimulating though sometimes difficult to accept. There are many references to Dickens throughout his writings.

PEARSON, H. *Dickens. His character, comedy, and career*. New York: Harper, 1949.

LINDSAY, JACK. *Charles Dickens*. A biographical and critical study. London: Dakers, 1950.

SYMONS, JULIAN. *Charles Dickens*. New York: Roy Publishers, 1951.

JOHNSON, EDGAR. *Charles Dickens: His Tragedy and Triumph*. New York: Simon and Schuster, 1953.
The best biography since Forster's of 1872–1874.

NISBET, ADA. *Dickens and Ellen Ternan*. Berkeley: University of California Press, 1952.
Included important new material.

MONOD, SYLVÈRE. *Dickens Romancier*. Paris: Hachette, 1953.
An important study of Dickens's methods as a novelist.

HOUSE, HUMPHRY. *All in Due Time*. London: Hart-Davis, 1955.
Includes "Part Three: Dickens."

FORD, G. H. *Dickens and His Readers. Aspects of Novel-Criticism since 1836*. Princeton: Princeton University Press, 1955.

ADRIAN, A. A. *Georgina Hogarth and the Dickens Circle*. New York: Oxford University Press, 1957.

FIELDING, K. J. *Charles Dickens: A Critical Introduction*. New York: McKay, 1958.

ZABEL, M. D. *Craft and Character in Modern Fiction*. New York: Viking, 1957.

BUTT, JOHN, AND TILLOTSON, KATHLEEN. *Dickens at Work*. London: Methuen, 1957.

MILLER, JOSEPH H. *Charles Dickens: The World of His Novels*. Cambridge: Harvard University Press, 1958.
Stimulating and thoughtful.

ENGEL, MONROE. *The Maturity of Dickens*. Cambridge: Harvard University Press, 1959.
Useful on the novel, politics, and *Our Mutual Friend*.

AYLMER, FELIX. *Dickens Incognito*. London: Hart-Davis, 1959.
About Dickens and Ellen Ternan. Definitely misleading as based on an admitted misreading of certain records: see London *Sunday Times*, December 13, 1959. Not to be completely ignored.

MANNING, JOHN. *Dickens on Education*. Toronto: University of Toronto Press, 1959.
Useful, but not the last word.

BUTT, JOHN (ed.). "A Dickens Symposium," *A Review of English Literature*, Vol. II (1961).

ROSE, W. CLARK (ed.). *Discussions of Charles Dickens*. Boston: Heath, 1961.
A useful, slim selection of previously published essays by modern critics.

COCKSHUT, A. O. J. *The Imagination of Charles Dickens*. New York: New York University Press, 1962.

COLLINS, PHILIP. *Dickens and Crime*. New York: St. Martin's, 1962.
An interesting work of scholarship offering new insights if applied to biography and criticism.

FORD, GEORGE, AND LANE, LAURIAT (eds.). *The Dickens Critics*. Ithaca: Cornell University Press, 1962.
An extremely useful selection of critical studies from Poe to Angus Wilson.

GROSS, JOHN, AND PEARSON, GABRIEL (eds.). *Dickens and the Twentieth Century*. Toronto: University of Toronto Press, 1962.
Twenty, mainly new essays giving a fresh survey of the novels.

SPILKA, M. *Dickens and Kafka*. Bloomington: Indiana University Press, 1962.
More Kafkan than Dickensian, it yields rewardingly to close study.

LEAVIS, F. R. "Dombey and Son," *Sewanee Review*, Vol. LXX (1962).
"There is a greater Dickens than the traditional cult has tended to realize."

FORD, G. H., and others. *Dickens Criticism: Past, Present, and Future Directions. A Symposium*. Cambridge, Mass.: Lesley College, 1963.
A useful, forward-looking survey.

BROWN, I. *Dickens in his Time*. New York: Nelson, 1963.

COLLINS, P. A. *Dickens and Education*. New York: St. Martin's, 1963.
Includes valuable new information.

DAVIS, E. *The Flint and the Flame: The Artistry of Charles Dickens*. Columbia: University of Missouri Press, 1963.

The Dickensian: A magazine for Dickens lovers and monthly record of the Dickens Fellowship, 1905—in progress.
Now published three times a year.

ANTHONY TROLLOPE

by Hugh Sykes Davies

ANTHONY TROLLOPE
From a drawing by 'Sem.'

ANTHONY TROLLOPE was born on April 24, 1815, in London. He died on December 6, 1882, at Harting, Sussex.

TROLLOPE

I

ANTHONY TROLLOPE was born in 1815. His father was a barrister, learned in law, but of difficult temper and unpractical in the management of his affairs. The first twenty years of his son's life were overshadowed by the gradual failure of the legal practice, and by a series of ill planned and worse executed manoeuvres to make money in other ways.

The ruin of the family was delayed, and at the last made less ruinous, by Anthony's mother, Frances Trollope. One of her husband's weirdest schemes was to set up a great bazaar in Cincinnati, and he despatched his wife to America to supervise its building, in a striking medley of classical and oriental styles. Funds were exhausted before it could be stocked with goods, and Mrs. Trollope found herself in penury. She learned from this crisis not only that she must herself take on a great part of the task of supporting her family, but also a possible means of performing it. On her return to England, she wrote her first book, a racy and rather acid study of the American way of life. It was successful, and she went on at once to write novels and other travelogues. When her husband finally became bankrupt in 1834, she took the family to Belgium, and supported them by her pen, never laying it aside for long, even while she saw to the housekeeping, and tended the deathbeds of her favourite son, her husband, and her youngest daughter. Her later days were happier and more prosperous, but she went on writing indefatigably when the financial need had passed. When she died, at the age of eighty-three, she had written forty-one books, and her annual rate of production had not been far below that achieved by Anthony himself. They were both late starters in literature: he was forty when his first book was published, and she fifty-two. For both of them, the first conscious aim in writing was to make money; but once started, they both found that it satisfied in them needs much deeper than that of money.

Possibly Trollope inherited from his mother some qualities of mind and spirit that favoured quick and copious writing, and certainly he had before him her example of what might be made of these qualities. But the deeper needs which writing came to satisfy were the unhappy by-product of his father's misfortunes. When he was seven, he went to Harrow as a day-boy. At twelve, he was moved to his father's old school, Winchester, but taken away three years later because the bills had not been paid, and could not be paid. Long before his departure, the other boys had known of the unpaid bills, and had made use of their knowledge. 'It is the nature of boys to be cruel,' he mildly observed of their doings when he wrote of them in later life. But worse was to follow, for he went back to Harrow again as a day-boy. By this time, his mother was in America, and he was living with his father, unkempt and uncouth, in a gloomy tumbledown farm-house, from which he tramped twice a day through muddy lanes to sit among the well fed and smartly dressed boarders. 'The indignities I endured are not to be described,' he wrote later. 'I was never able to over-come—or even attempt to overcome—the absolute isolation of my school position. Of the cricket-ground or racket-court I was allowed to know nothing. And yet I longed for these things with an exceeding great longing. I coveted popularity with a coveting which was almost mean. It seemed to me that there would be an Elysium in the intimacy of those very boys I was bound to hate because they hated me. Something of the disgrace of my school-days has clung to me all through life.'

He was removed from Harrow at last by the bankruptcy of his father, and went with the rest of the family to Bel-gium, a useless and aimless witness of their successive deaths. At the age of nineteen, however, he was wangled by family friends into the Post Office as a junior clerk; competitive examinations to the Civil Service being still to come. In later life, he wrote and spoke vehemently against that mode of recruitment, on the ground that it would certainly have excluded him, and that the Service would have lost a good official by his exclusion. Probably he was right on both points, yet it would not have been easy for any department to function with more than one or two Anthony Trollopes on its strength. He was unpunctual and insubordinate, and he got into 'scrapes'. Once, in an argument with the secretary, he banged a table so hard that it catapulted an inkwell into his chief's face: since the Post Office was at that time ruled by a retired Colonel, he was lucky to have escaped dismissal or something worse. And one day the office was invaded by a lady under a vast bonnet, with a basket on her arm, crying loudly 'Anthony Trollope, when are you going to marry my daughter?' He did not have to marry the young lady, but he admitted that 'these little incidents were all against me in the office'.

This period of his life lasted for seven years, and it is the one period of which he has told us very little. He lived in poor lodgings, spent much time in bars, got into debt and made his one and only acquaintance with a money-lender. He began, however, to make friends, and after the disgrace of his schooldays, it was much to him that men of his own age were willing to like him, to talk with him, and to spend their week-ends walking with him. In the office, he kept his place, largely because he turned out to be very good at writing letters, and in the end even his 'scrapes' did him a backhanded service, for the ink-stained Colonel recommended him for a job in Ireland, as the best way to be rid of him.

It was a very great service, however backhanded. Ireland accomplished a transformation in him hardly less dramatic than that which characterizes the life-cycles of insects. Hitherto, his state had been dark and larval, or chrysalid at best, and his days had been spent in obscurity and lonely poverty. 'From the day on which I set foot in Ireland,' he wrote, 'all these evils fell away from me. Since that time who has had a happier life than mine?' The essence of the Irish magic was that for the first time he found himself among people who liked him, who did not regard him as a shameful and useless encumbrance. The work was not in an office under superiors, but in the open air on his own, riding up and down, making arrangements or putting disarrangements to rights. He became good at the work itself, and passionately fond of riding. He took to hunting, and found a hobby that was his only major addiction to the end of his life. After three years of this new life, he married, was promoted, and soon began to write his first novel.

He spent most of his time in Ireland until 1859, and remained in the Post Office until 1867. He rose from being an ill-reputed and difficult clerk to being an efficient but still rather difficult public servant, with a flair for negotiating with all kinds of people, of many nations. He had a fine eye for the practical—he was the inventor of the English pillar-box. Above all, he made himself useful to his department in ways which meant that he was kept on his travels, rather than in an office. He came to know many parts of Britain itself, and visited Egypt, America and the West Indies on postal business. He hunted two days a week, and became a haunter of London clubs, partly for the sake of whist, partly because his acquaintance was now reaching up into higher circles of society and letters. And on top of all this, he wrote books at the average rate of 1·7 per annum, and made money by them.

So, in middle life, he found all that he had missed as a boy—respect, friendship and worldly success. And he enjoyed it all, hugely and noisily. He banged about the world, rode about Essex and other hunting counties, fell off his horse and lost his spectacles and laughed: dined at the club and laughed: dined at home or with his friends and laughed. In 1882, he was laughing at a comic book read aloud with his family after dinner when he had a stroke, from which he died a month later.

He had been successful, and had valued his success all the more because of his early failures. 'To be known as somebody,' he wrote, 'to be Anthony Trollope—if it be no more —is to me much.' But to understand both the man and his work, it is needful to set this beside that other verdict: 'Something of the disgrace of my schooldays has clung to me all through life.'

II

The above quotations are all from Trollope's *Autobiography*, written in 1875-6, but not published until 1883, a year after his death. Its reputation has kept pace with the recent revival of respect for his novels, and it is now probably one of the most widely read of English autobiographies. This modest popularity it well deserves. As an account of his life, it is so complete and so just that his biographers have added little to its detail, and less to its broad outline. It is in no sense a work of intimate self-revelation, and was not intended to be. It is rather a *tour de force* of self-description by a man who, sitting for his own portrait, brought to it precisely the same technique of direct solidity which he had developed in painting scores of portraits in his novels. He did not even spare himself the slightly ironic distance from which he usually observed his male characters. And what it describes is not merely an attitude taken up for the occasion, but one which served him constantly for the more serious purposes of self-regard.

Yet the self-portrait is a little uneven, clearly delineated where his habitual perceptions were strong, but fainter and more confused where they were weak. His strength lay in describing the manners and morals of the world in which he was so anxious to bear—and even more anxious to deserve—a good name; and in his account of his dealings with this world, he has a natural rightness and honesty which enabled him to behave well, and to describe clearly. His moral standards were not, perhaps, very profound or very subtle, but they were worthy and workable, and they made his conduct better than that of many men who were his superiors in moral perception. His weakness lay rather in his attitude to his own writing, and to literature in general. Here he fell into confusions and distortions which have harmed his reputation and—what is worse—damaged his work.

The problem for him lay in a simple contradiction. On the one hand, he was trying to rise in the world by writing novels; on the other hand, the world into which he wished to rise did not have a high regard for novels, or for those who wrote them. 'Thinking much', he said, 'of my own daily labour and of its nature, I felt myself at first to be much afflicted and then to be deeply grieved by the opinion expressed by wise and thinking men as to the work done by novelists.' To this problem, he found two possible answers. Very early in his career as a novelist he proposed to write a history of English prose fiction, which was to have 'vindicated my own profession as a novelist' by demonstrating in the work of his predecessors and contemporaries 'that high character which they may claim to have earned by their grace, their honesty, and good teaching'. But this history was never written, though a few of its leading ideas are suggested briefly in Chapters 12 and 13 of the *Autobiography*. The other possible answer, on the contrary, was made fully, loudly and insistently, throughout the book. It was that novel-writing should be regarded as a profession like any other, and that the object of the novelist, like that of every other professional man, was to make money for himself and his dependants. Nor was this object an unworthy or base one. 'It is a mistake,' he wrote, 'to suppose that a man is a better man because he despises money. Few do so, and those few in doing so suffer a defect. Who does not desire to be hospitable to his friends, generous to the poor, liberal to all, munificent to his children, and to be himself free from the carking fears which poverty creates?' This was the answer to which he committed himself, and it was elaborated in almost every account he gave of his dealings with publishers, up to the last page of the *Autobiography*, with its detailed financial statement of his earnings from each of his books, meticulously totalled to £68,939.17.5.

It was, perhaps, the answer most likely to impress the world which he sought to impress. The men he met in the hunting field, or over the card table at his club, were more likely to accept it than that other argument about the good done by novelists in the moral education of their readers; and they were more likely to welcome among them a professional man just such as they were themselves—barristers, clergymen, engineers—who made no claim to be doing more than earn a good living. But though it was perhaps well fitted for this purpose, it was wrong, even perversely wrong. The novelist is not, of course, exempt from the common necessity of earning a living. But he earns it as a novelist, rather than as a barrister, a clergyman, an engineer, a politician or a confidence-trickster, because his tastes and abilities carry him to the novel rather than to any of these other lucrative activities. Yet although Trollope could not, or would not see this, it is typical of him that he gave a faithful report of the manner in which his own tastes and abilities were turned in this direction. Writing of those disgraced schooldays, and of the hardly less disgraced years as a clerk in the Post Office, he said this:

> I was always going about with some castles in the air firmly built within my mind. Nor were these efforts at architecture spasmodic or subject to constant change from day to day. For weeks, for months, if I remember rightly, from year to year, I would carry on the same tale, binding myself down to certain laws, to certain proportions. Nothing impossible was ever introduced,—nor anything which, from outward circumstances, would seem to be violently improbable. This had been the occupation of my life for six or seven years before I went to the Post Office, and was by no

means abandoned when I commenced my work. There can, I imagine, hardly be a more dangerous mental practice; but I have often doubted whether, had it not been my practice, I should ever have written a novel. I learned in this way to maintain an interest in a fictitious story, to dwell on a work created by my own imagination, and to live in a world altogether outside the world of my own material life.

It is here, and not in the passages on money-making, that Trollope describes his real impulse to write novels. He became a writer, not because of his need for money, but because of his talent for imaginative day-dreams. It was natural that he should have confused the need with the talent, for both drew their strength from the same source. The former was a conscious passion, almost an obsession, because it was the outward symbol of his desire to rise above those early outward troubles, and the latter also was passionate, but more obscurely, because it had been his hidden inner resource against them. The confusion was natural, but none the less unfortunate. At first it prevented him from discovering where his true gift lay, and even after this discovery, he under-rated its value in himself. In deference to the standards of the hunting-field and the club, he abused and exploited it by writing too much and too quickly, without waiting for his imagination to gather weight and depth. Like some of the more enterprising bankers of his time, he possessed genuine gold, but made it serve to support a recklessly diffuse paper circulation.

III

Misconceiving both his own powers and the nature of fiction, Trollope fell an easy prey to the shallower notions of his age about the way novels should be written. It was his job, he supposed, as an honest professional man, to provide his customers with the commodity they expected; and what they expected, he was taught to believe, was 'realism', slices of life faithfully observed and entertainingly told, with a few touches of wholesome morality. When he first resolved to write a novel, the life that lay under his eyes was that of Ireland, so he cut a few slices from it, observed them industriously, and wrote them down as best he could. His two Irish novels were failures, as they deserved to be. An historical novel followed, as dismally cluttered up with book-learning as the Irish novels had been by unimaginative reporting. Then he tried his hand at a guide-book, but the publishers to whom specimens were sent omitted to read them, and the project was dropped.

He was turned from these false starts, from his conception of the novel as a mere animated guide-book, not by any growth of literary perception on his own part, but by a lucky accident of his official career. In 1851 he was given the task of organizing country posts in South-West England, and for two happy years he rode up and down and about in six or seven counties, visiting many places, meeting many people, but always in a hurry. It was his first experience of England outside London, and its combination of variety and hurry was exactly what his imagination needed to work upon; the materials offered to it were extensive, but he moved too quickly to become bogged down anywhere. From these wanderings, he got, not another careful slice of life, but a hazy, rich impression of towns and villages, of churches and country houses, of clergy and laity, and of the quietly intricate patterns of their manners and social life. It was upon this impression that he based his first truly imaginative novel, *The Warden*, the first of that Barsetshire series which has come to be regarded as his highest achievement. The book was conceived one summer evening in Salisbury, but the Barchester of the novels was never merely Salisbury, nor was the county round it any one of the counties through which he had travelled. It was pieced together from memories of them all, and though it grew to be so clear in his head that he once drew a very detailed map of it, its solidity was imaginative, not geographical. In the same way, the clergy who were its main characters were not of his acquaintance. 'I never,' he tells us in the *Autobiography*, 'lived in any cathedral city,—except London, never knew anything of any Close, and at that time had enjoyed no peculiar intimacy with any clergyman. My archdeacon, who has been said to be life-like, and for whom I confess I have all a parent's fond affection, was, I think, the simple result of an effort of my moral consciousness. . . . I had not then ever spoken to an archdeacon.' Similarly, the great journalist Tom Towers was thought to be very like an eminent man on the staff of *The Times*, and *The Times* itself, in its review of *The Warden*, mildly rebuked the author for indulging in personalities. But at that time, Trollope protests, 'living in Ireland, I had not even heard the name of any gentleman connected with *The Times* newspaper, and could not have intended to represent any individual by Tom Towers. As I had created an archdeacon, so I had created a journalist . . . my moral consciousness must again have been very powerful.'

This gift for the creation of character by the use of his moral imagination was revealed for the first time in *The Warden*, but it had been developed through those long years of day-dreaming, and in its own rather unusual direction. His private fantasies had not been adventurous, nor had they conferred upon him glittering social status. 'I never became a king,' he tells us, 'or a duke . . . a learned man, nor even a philosopher. But I was a very clever person, and beautiful young women used to be fond of me. And I strove to be kind of heart, and open of hand, and noble in thought, despising mean things; and altogether I was a very much better fellow than I have ever succeeded in being since.' This passionate and genuinely imaginative concern with moral existence was the essence of his approach to the novel, from *The Warden* onwards. Above all, it was his chief means of insight into character and its depiction. The physical characteristics of his personages are rarely made clearly visible, though they are often conscientiously described. It is their moral physiognomies that are sharply drawn, through what they do and say, what they are said to think and feel, and not seldom by direct comments upon them from their maker.

In the type of moral character chosen for portrayal, *The Warden* set the pattern to which he kept in nearly all his later novels. There was no villain, indeed no character much below the middle range of the moral scale, nor was there anyone conspicuously above it, save the Warden himself. Trollope became exactly what he wished, the moral historian of men and women in the middle range, the usual run of humanity—'with no more of excellence, nor with exaggerated baseness—so that my readers might recognize human beings like to themselves, and not feel themselves to be carried away among gods or demons'.

Finally, *The Warden* was typical of all the novels that were to follow in its disregard for plot. It would, indeed, have been incompatible with his choice of the middle range of characters to have involved them in sensational and complicated situations: ordinary people commonly lead ordinary lives. But apart from this, the elaboration of remarkable incident was quite irrelevant to his main purpose—the depiction of moral character. It mattered little to him how his creatures were set in motion, for once they were on the move they had so great a capacity for living their own lives. In *The Warden* itself, he posed them a problem about the proper use of church endowments, a contemporary, if not a burning issue: just such a case had arisen in Winchester when he was at school there, and was still before the courts many years after he had written this book. But he himself had no clear view of its rights and wrongs, nor did he need one. All that he needed was the opportunity to let his imagination play upon its issues and cross-issues, as they would appear to differing modes and degrees of moral sensibility. And it was in the process of doing this that men and women—not issues—came alive under his hand.

IV

The intense moral realization of his characters gave them, once created, a very tenacious hold upon his imagination: so tenacious that he was often unwilling, almost unable, to let them go. His two most notable creations in *The Warden* were of this kind, and they were carried on into *Barchester Towers* (1857), *Doctor Thorne* (1858), *Framley Parsonage* (1861) and *The Last Chronicle of Barset* (1867). Other characters were added, of course, and some of them obtained almost as close a grip on their author's affections. Other novels were written in the same period, many of them. But Archdeacon Grantly and his father-in-law went on leading their lives in his imagination, growing older as he grew older, yet always themselves as he remained himself. Of the two, the Archdeacon was the more prominent and active, and much more akin to Trollope. His father-in-law, who had been Warden in the first book, stood at the upper limit of Trollope's moral range, and once he had made his great decision in that first episode, there was little for him to do in the world but be gentle to his family and friends, play his 'cello, and take good care of the music in the cathedral. Yet he did all this in such a way that we are made to feel his virtue, his religion even, beyond any description that Trollope felt able to give. The Archdeacon was coarser in grain, quick to anger, but quick to forget his anger, more worldly, but generous and warm-hearted. The two existed side by side, as characters must often do in fiction, making a richer pattern by their contrasting qualities than they could ever have made separately. When the older man came to die, it was through the mouth of the Archdeacon that Trollope expressed his estimate both of the dying man, and of the Archdeacon:

> I feel sure that he never had an impure fancy in his mind, or a faulty wish in his heart. His tenderness has surpassed the tenderness of woman; and yet, when occasion came for showing it, he had all the spirit of a hero. I shall never forget his resignation of the

hospital. . . . The fact is, he never was wrong. He couldn't go wrong. He lacked guile, and he feared God,—and a man who does both will never go far astray. I don't think he ever coveted aught in his life,—except a new case for his violoncello and somebody to listen to him when he played it. Then the archdeacon got up, and walked about the room in his enthusiasm; and, perhaps, as he walked some thoughts as to the sterner ambition of his own life passed through his mind. What things had he coveted? Had he lacked guile? He told himself that he had feared God,—but he was not sure that he was telling himself the truth even in that.

Nothing is more like Trollope himself than this moment of explosive self-perception. The Archdeacon, like his creator, had standards by which to measure his fellow men, and he was tolerably sure of their general rightness. But when he came to ask how far he himself measured up to them, he had his awkward moments. He had coveted many things, greatly: a Bishopric, power, the ruin of his enemies, wealth, and above all in his later days, the glory of his children. He had indeed done his best for them, and they had not done badly for him. His daughter was a marchioness, and though her husband the marquis was unquestionably a moron, she was still unquestionably a marchioness. His eldest son, Henry, had done well in the Indian Army, had won the Victoria Cross, and a wife with a little money. The wife had died, leaving the young widower with a baby daughter, but Henry still had his fine record, some money of his own, and a handsome allowance with his father. He had retired from the Army, and was settling in Barsetshire as a country squire, with land and farms and horses and foxes of his own.

All this had been achieved by stern ambition, and not without guile; and whatever God might think about it, the Archdeacon was usually well pleased with his achievements. In *The Last Chronicle of Barset*, he was sorely tried because Henry fell deeply in love with a young woman, the daughter of a cleric the very opposite of himself, pious, very poor, unworldly, and to make the worst of an already bad job, awaiting his trial on a charge of stealing a cheque. So outrageous was Henry's choice, that his father opposed this new marriage, even threatened to stop the allowance. The struggle between father and son was long and obstinate on both sides, and even the mother's intervention was not able to end it. It was brought to its climax, and at the same instant to its solution, in an interview between the Archdeacon and the girl herself, which illustrates as comprehensively as any passage in Trollope both the emotional force of which he was capable, and the moral standards which he accepted without question. The first part of the interview does her credit—more credit than the Archdeacon had expected. She refers to her father's disgrace, and gives her promise that unless his name is cleared, she will marry nobody:

> The archdeacon had now left the rug, and advanced till he was almost close to the chair on which Grace was sitting. 'My dear,' he said, 'what you say does you very much honour—very much honour indeed.' Now that he was close to her, he could look into her eyes, and he could see the exact form of her features, and could understand—could not help understanding—the character of her countenance. It was a noble face, having in it nothing that was poor, nothing that was mean, nothing that was shapeless. It was a face that promised infinite beauty, with a promise that was on the very verge of fulfilment. There was a play about her mouth as she spoke, and a curl in her nostrils as the eager words came from her, which almost made the selfish father give way. Why had they not told him that she was such a one as this? Why had not Henry himself spoken of the speciality of her beauty? No man in England knew better than the archdeacon the difference between beauty of one kind and beauty of another kind in a woman's face—the one beauty, which comes from health and youth and animal spirits, and which belongs to the miller's daughter, and the other beauty, which shows itself in fine lines and a noble spirit—the beauty which comes from breeding. 'What you say does you very much honour indeed,' said the archdeacon.
> 'I should not mind at all about being poor,' said Grace.
> 'No; no; no,' said the archdeacon.

'Poor as we are—and no clergyman, I think, ever was so poor—I should have done as your son asked me at once, if it had been only that—because I love him.'

'If you love him you will not wish to injure him.'

'I will not injure him. Sir, there is my promise.' And now as she spoke she rose from her chair, and standing close to the archdeacon, laid her hand very lightly on the sleeve of his coat. 'There is my promise. As long as people say that papa stole the money, I will never marry your son. There.'

The archdeacon was still looking down at her, and feeling the slight touch of her fingers, raised his arm a little as though to welcome the pressure. He looked into her eyes, which were turned eagerly towards his, and when doing so he was sure that the promise would be kept. It would have been sacrilege—he felt that it would have been sacrilege—to doubt such a promise. He almost relented. His soft heart, which was never very well under his own control, gave way so far that he was nearly moved to tell her that, on his son's behalf, he acquitted her of the promise. . . . As he looked down upon her face two tears formed themselves in his eyes and gradually trickled down his old nose. 'My dear,' he said, 'if this cloud passes away from you, you shall come to us and be my daughter.' And thus he pledged himself. There was a dash of generosity about the man, in spite of his selfishness, which always made him desirous of giving largely to those who gave largely to him. He would fain that his gifts should be bigger, if it were possible. . . . He had contrived that her hand should fall from his arm into his grasp, and now for a moment he held it. 'You are a good girl,' he said—'a dear, dear, good girl. When this cloud has passed away, you shall come to us and be our daughter.'

It was thus that Trollope created the most solid of his male characters, by a temporary merging of his own personality in theirs: here, he has all but put himself into the Archdeacon's shoes and gaiters. But the merging was never uncritical, because he was critical of himself; he was always capable of qualifying a virtue, of noting an unworthy doubt, and took frequent pleasure in slight backhanded ironies at the expense of their inner weaknesses, as he did at the expense of his own.

As for the girls, he was inclined to be in love with them

in the same vicarious fashion. His contemporaries, we are informed by a review written in 1867, liked to make gentle jokes about his intimacy with the minds of his heroines: how, they asked, had he managed to 'find it all out'? And shortly after his death, Henry James accurately noted the nature of his relation with them:

> Trollope settled down steadily to the English girl; he took possession of her, and turned her inside out. He never made her the subject of heartless satire . . . he bestowed upon her the most serious, the most patient, the most tender, the most copious consideration. He is evidently always more or less in love with her. . . . But if he was a lover, he was a paternal lover.

It was, indeed, the English girl who saved Trollope from the labour of devising plots. She was there to be loved, and love for her was enough to set in motion not only one or two young men, but their families too. For only if the love went hand in hand with an income large enough to support marriage—and marriage in the style to which both parties were accustomed—could it run all smooth. All that was needful, then, to produce a story with situations full of doubt and perplexity was to bring the power of love into conflict with the demands of property and social status. The ensuing confusion would involve not only the lovers, but their families and friends, and as wide a circle of acquaintance as might be needed to fill a three volume novel. Trollope made this discovery early in the Barsetshire series, and thenceforward he never bothered his head with plots. 'When I sit down to write a novel', he blandly observed, 'I do not at all know, and I do not very much care, how it is to end.' For this relief, he was almost entirely indebted to the English girl with her ability to inspire love, and to the Victorian sense of property with its inveterate tendency to make love injudicious. As the great tragic conflicts in French classical plays tend to arise from the opposition of love and honour, so Trollope's arose from love and property.

But it would be unjust to present him as becoming thus involved only with young lovers, or with characters on the whole amiable and admirable. Such was his involvement in any creation of his own that he was almost equally capable of becoming devoted to personages neither young nor amiable. In the Barsetshire novels, for example, the Archdeacon's arch-enemy is Mrs. Proudie, wife of the Bishop and mistress of the palace which the Archdeacon had coveted so much, and which his father had held before him. Mrs. Proudie is probably the best-known virago in English fiction, above all for her achievements in hen-pecking her husband, yet even to her Trollope developed a powerful attachment. The manner of her death was curious. One night at his club, he heard two clergymen criticizing him for carrying the same characters from novel to novel, and they were very hard on Mrs. Proudie. 'I got up, and standing between them, I acknowledged myself to be the culprit. "As to Mrs. Proudie," I said, "I will go home and kill her before the week is over." And so I did . . . but I have never dissevered myself from Mrs. Proudie, and still live much in company with her ghost.'

V

The Barsetshire novels have come to be regarded as Trollope's chief, if not his only contribution to literature, both by the common reader and by the general run of critics and literary historians. They hold this position partly through their own merits of character and milieu, but partly because they can so easily be made to satisfy the common reader's most common weakness in his choice of fiction, his liking for some more or less adult fairyland where he can take a well earned holiday from the tougher and duller realities of his own life. 'Barset,' J. B. Priestley has observed, 'is a haven of rest.' It is natural enough that novels whose main setting was rural England, and whose main characters were so often country clergy, should have been appreciated in this way. But it is an injustice to this series of novels to perceive in them no more than pleasant placidity, and it can easily lead on to a still greater injustice in estimating Trollope's work. For the more solid qualities in this series are to be found in many of his other novels, where the milieu is less obviously fairy-like, but where his central virtue of moral imagination shows itself both with greater depth and with wider range.

These qualities are nowhere more massively developed than in the linked series of novels which ran through his later life, much as the Barsetshire series had run through his earlier years, the 'political' novels, whose central characters are Plantagenet Palliser and his wife Glencora: *Can You Forgive Her?* (1864), *Phineas Finn* (1869), *The Eustace Diamonds* (1873), *Phineas Redux* (1874), *The Prime Minister* (1876) and *The Duke's Children* (1880).

The main setting has moved from Barsetshire to London, and the main characters are men of wealth and high social status, leaders in their professions and in the House of Commons. The general impression is one of greater 'realism', at any rate in so far as this world is clearly more remote from any conceivable fairyland than Barsetshire had been. But in following Trollope's achievement in this less idyllic milieu, it is even more necessary to realize how much it issued from his imagination. It had been the dread of his boyhood, as he walked to Harrow along the muddy lanes, that 'mud and solitude and poverty' would be his lot through his whole life. 'Those lads about me would go into Parliament, or become rectors and deans, or squires of parishes, or advocates thundering at the Bar,' he supposed; and he told himself that he would never live among them. But with the success of his middle years, he had after all risen to live among them. He knew Members of Parliament, thundering barristers, and the brother of his closest friend was Dean of Ely. And in 1868, he tried to rise still higher, by standing as a candidate for Parliament himself, at Beverley. He was defeated, and both the fact and the manner of his defeat left a very sore place in his spirit. But if he could rise no further himself, his imagination could go where it liked, and its expeditions were the main impulse of the political novels. This was his own view of them—and as usual he saw himself with accuracy:

> By no amount of description or asseveration could I succeed in making any reader understand how much these characters (Palliser and Lady Glencora) with their belongings have been to me in my latter life; or how frequently I have used them for the expression of my political and social convictions. They have been as real to me as free trade was to Mr. Cobden, or the dominion of a party to Mr. Disraeli; and as I have not been able to speak from the benches of the House of Commons . . . they have served me as safety valves by which to deliver my soul.

In this way, his defeat at Beverley gave him a new imaginative impulse, and at the same time ensured that his imagination would not get itself bogged down in too much minute observation. His acquaintance with the political world, like his earlier survey of south-west England, was both wide and vague enough to give him precisely the kind of rich but hazy impression which left his imagination neither starved nor shackled.

In the political novels, as in the earlier series, there is a vast array of characters, and most of them are set and kept in motion by Trollope's usual forces, love and property. But in the central character, Plantagenet Palliser, the chief interest is subtler and deeper. It is a long, full study of a conscience, delicate in itself, and even more perplexed because its owner has wealth, a dukedom, political power, and a very thin skin. The close of *The Prime Minister* is a good example of what Trollope's 'moral consciousness' could make of this material. Palliser has been Prime Minister for three years, as head of a coalition Government. When it falls, his old friend and ally, the Duke of St. Bungay, expresses the hope that he will take some office in the next Cabinet. 'I don't think I could do that,' Palliser told him,

'Caesar could hardly lead a legion under Pompey.' But when their talk was over, he found himself regretting 'that apparently pompous speech about Caesar. . . . Who was he that he should class himself among the great ones of the world.' In the days that followed, this moment of unintended arrogance irked him almost more than the end of his power and the formation of a new administration. A few weeks later, he was talking with his late Chancellor of the Exchequer, one of the few political allies he respected, and by him he was given this assurance:

> 'If the country is to lose your services for the long course of years during which you will probably sit in Parliament, then I shall think that the country has lost more than it has gained by the Coalition.'
>
> The Duke sat for a while silent, looking at the view, and, before answering Mr. Monk,—while arranging his answer,—once or twice in a half-absent way called his companion's attention to the scene before him. But, during this time he was going through an act of painful repentance. He was condemning himself for a word or two that had been ill-spoken by himself, and which, since the moment of its utterance, he had never ceased to remember with shame. He told himself now, after his own secret fashion, that he must do penance for these words by the humiliation of a direct contradiction of them. He must declare that Caesar would at some future time be prepared to serve under Pompey. Thus he made his answer.

This is a more interesting process of the moral life than any studied in the Barset novels, and the observation is more penetrating: few moralists have noted so clearly the part which a small phrase, almost a chance phrase, can play in bringing the fluid confusions of the inner life to a point where they crystallize into decision.

But the fine conscience of Plantagenet Palliser is more than an individual study. It is also at the centre of Trollope's political world, and he finds in it the explanation of a process of change in England which was otherwise mystifying. He was himself a Liberal, though with many touches of the

Tory in his temperament. He approved in general of the slow process of amelioration which was going on in his day, the gradual spread of democracy and of education to wider sections of the population. He even approved of the extension of the franchise, but at the same time he wondered at the fact that some of the great Whigs, especially those of wealth and title, should be willing to use their political influence for its own destruction, by encouraging it to pass into the hands of millions of men with votes to be cast in secret ballot. Palliser is the type of such a Whig, and in his exact and exacting conscience Trollope finds the explanation of this remarkable change. No other English novelist, and few historians, saw the problem so clearly, and advanced so convincing a solution for it.

It is this extension of his 'moral consciousness' to the whole pattern of English life that informs the political novels, and justifies to the full the remarkable tribute which Henry James paid Trollope a few years after his death:

> Trollope will remain one of the most trustworthy, though not one of the most eloquent, of writers who have helped the heart of man to know itself. . . . His natural rightness and purity are so real that the good things he projects must be real. A race is fortunate when it has a good deal of the sort of imagination—of imaginative feeling—that had fallen to the share of Anthony Trollope; and in this possession our English race is not poor.

VI

Trollope wrote forty-seven novels, and since few readers will wish to read them all, some answer is needed to the question, which are best worth reading? It is not easy to find one, for quite apart from the large number involved, there are few that fall markedly below his usual level, and perhaps even fewer which rise much above it.

The verdict of the common reader has always been that the Barset series should be regarded as his best and most typical work, and that there is little point in going much further with him. His more serious and persistent readers, however, generally believe that the 'political' series is at least as good, and very probably better. Beyond this, there is confusion. Are the other three dozen novels merely an extension of the Trollopian world over a wider area, a repetition of his favourite themes and his familiar types of character under new names and against slightly shifted scenery? Or do some of them present qualities not to be found anywhere in the two central series?

The second argument has been urged with much force in a recent study by Mr. Cockshut, which sets out to alter radically the accepted view of Trollope's whole work. It contends that Trollope's outlook was, especially in the later part of his life, much less superficial than has usually been supposed, less orthodox, less bluffly optimistic, and more prone to question the assumptions of the age about morality and property. In the light of this contention, the emphasis of attention is changed both within the two main series and in the novels outside them. In the Barset novels, it falls above all on the lonely agony of Mr. Crawley, the clergyman wrongly accused of stealing a cheque, but not sure within himself that he is innocent. In the 'political' series, it falls upon the madness of Mr. Kennedy in *Phineas Finn* and *Phineas Redux*, and the appalling loneliness of his wife, Lady Laura, who has married him for his money—or at least refused to marry the man she really loved because he had no money. And in *The Eustace Diamonds*, Mr. Cockshut finds Trollope's first decisive movement towards satire, and to a view of goods and chattels not wholeheartedly Victorian. With this alteration of emphasis in the better-known novels, there goes the claim that what is most important in them was often more fully developed elsewhere. The gloom and loneliness of the individual, for example, was explored most deeply in *He Knew He Was Right*, which traces the degeneration of a husband from unreasonable jealousy of his wife into actual madness. The fullest development of satire is in *The Way We Live Now*, and of the attack on property and inheritance in *Mr. Scarborough's Family*. These, and other of the outlying novels, Mr. Cockshut would place in the forefront of Trollope's work, for these and such-like reasons.

This study has been usefully done; it provokes a more careful reading of some perhaps unduly neglected novels in the later period, and corrects some wrong impressions about those which have been widely read. Mr. Cockshut, moreover, has drawn together very skilfully the evidence of Trollope's passionate interest in certain situations and characters: the almost inevitably bad relations between fathers and sons, the 'snarling intimacy of family life', the desperation of girls whose only future is marriage, and whose labour in life is to entrap a suitably endowed husband. And yet the direction of the emphasis is wrong; it runs too directly against the main current of criticism. In his own day, Trollope's reviewers constantly stressed his choice of the middle range of humanity, of the ordinary man or woman, even the commonplace; they only wondered at his power of making it interesting, without distortion and without much apparent imaginative heightening of colour. Henry James's phrase succinctly comprehends the whole contemporary impression: 'His great, his inestimable merit was a complete appreciation of the usual.' The judgement is the more weighty, because a writer's contemporaries very rarely mistake the nature of his merit, though they often misjudge its degree. In concentrating so much attention upon Trollope's handling of the unusual, the heterodox, Mr. Cockshut has indulged in an exaggeration, even if a useful one.

My own conviction is that all the essential qualities of Trollope are to be found in the two central series, and that there they are balanced in their right proportions. Outside them, only two novels appear to me to have a really strong claim on the general reader.

The first is *The Way We Live Now*. It was written in

1873, and it savagely satirized the new power of financiers and speculators in English life. Trollope saw them compassing the ruin, or at least the degradation, of the landed gentry, literature, the press, social life, even the Court itself. It is a magnificently sustained piece of anger, imaginatively realized and dramatically presented. The last act of its great villain, Augustus Melmotte, ruined, drunk and defiant, trying to speak in Parliament, and glowering angrily but speechlessly round the House, has a force, both immediate and symbolic, beyond Trollope's usual range. In the previous year, *The Prime Minister* had appeared, and in it the new corruption of finance had been represented by a small-scale swindler, Lopez. Had Trollope but waited for his imagination to devise and select, he might have put the far greater figure of Melmotte in the same place. A novel in which Plantagenet Palliser was opposed to Melmotte, politically, morally and imaginatively, would in all probability have been Trollope's unquestioned masterpiece, his most complete comment on the values of his age. That it did not get written is the heaviest single penalty he paid for his precipitation in covering the daily stint of paper. But even so, *The Way We Live Now* deserves to be read more widely, and to be allowed a distinguished place beside the main political novels.

The second novel which I would specially commend is *The Claverings*, published in 1867. It is a work of a very different kind. It is short, and has a concentration of effect unusual in Trollope. There is no sub-plot to distract the development of the central situation, and all the characters play real parts in it. The main problem it explores, the hesitations and weaknesses of a young man between a beautiful but poor young girl to whom he is engaged, and an equally beautiful but rich widow whom he had loved before her marriage, is exactly of the kind to display at its best Trollope's ability to analyse the unheroic but not quite base man of common mould. But it is above all in its style that it is distinctive. For the most part, Trollope's manner

of writing is adequate rather than eloquent, and so impersonal that one often feels it might have been practised by
almost anyone else in the same period: though it is remarkable how surely, in fact, a fair specimen of his work can be
recognized for what it is. In *The Claverings*, however, more
than in any other book, he showed what he could do when
he was neither writing against the clock, nor merely 'for
length'—the dreadful phrase is his own. It is not merely that
as a whole the book is better written than most of the
others, but that it also shows some of his subtler qualities
of style more clearly than the rest.

There is, for example, a turn of phrase almost peculiar to
him, and very characteristic of his ironically intimate report
of the inner life: it depends upon the addition of some slight
qualification to a previous statement. An example has been
given already from the Archdeacon's reflections:

> He told himself that he had feared God,—but he was not sure
> that he was telling himself the truth even in that.

Here are others:

> He thought that he could give up racecourses; but he was sure
> that he could at any rate say that he would give them up. (*Sir Harry
> Hotspur of Humblethwaite.*)
>
> Colonel Osborne knew that his visit had been very innocent;
> but he did not like the feeling that even his innocence had been
> made the subject of observation. (*He Knew He Was Right.*)
>
> It cannot be said of him that he did much thinking for himself;—
> but he thought that he thought. (*The Prime Minister.*)

In *The Claverings*, this characteristic Trollopian turn of
phrase is used frequently, and especially in the depiction
of the wavering hero. 'He told himself that he was an ass,
but still he went on being an ass.' Thus he got himself into
his trouble between the old love and the new, and in the
midst of it, when he was being true to neither, Trollope
concludes an address to the reader on the failings of his hero:
'He should have been chivalric, manly, full of high duty.
He should have been all this, and full also of love, and then

he would have been a hero. But men as I see them are not often heroic.'

Another of Trollope's characteristic devices was the repetition of a short phrase, at brief intervals but with such shifts of context, such exaggeration, that it acquired the ironic power conferred in the same manner on the phrase 'honourable men' in Antony's speech in *Julius Caesar*. In *The Claverings*, there are two fine examples of its use. One is in the twelfth chapter, describing the visit of the beautiful young widow to the splendid estate she had won by her loveless marriage, and the phrase woven through it is 'She had the price in her hands'. It gathers weight continually through the chapter, which ends upon the final bitter variation: 'She had the price in her hands, but she felt herself tempted to do as Judas did, to go out and hang herself.' Five chapters later, the same device is put to more openly comic and hostile uses, when the best mode of wooing this same rich young widow is discussed by Captain Clavering and Captain Boodle, after dinner at their club:

> 'Well, now, Clavvy, I'll tell you what my ideas are. When a man's trying a young filly, his hands can't be too light. A touch too much will bring her on her haunches, and throw her out of step. She should hardly feel the iron in her mouth. But when I've got to do with a trained mare, I always choose that she shall know that I'm there! Do you understand me?"
>
> 'Yes; I understand you, Doodles.'
>
> 'I always choose that she should know I'm there.' And Captain Boodle, as he repeated these manly words with a firm voice, put out his hands as though he were handling the horse's rein.

After the phrase has been relished a further half-dozen times, Boodle leaves his friend alone to meditate upon it:

> He sat the whole evening in the smoking-room, very silent, drinking slowly iced gin-and-water; and the more he drank the more assured he felt that he now understood the way in which he was to attempt the work before him. 'Let her know I'm there', he said to himself, shaking his head gently, so that no one should

observe him; 'yes, let her know I'm there.' Everything was contained in that precept. And he, with his hands before him on his knees, went through the process of steadying a horse with the snaffle-rein, just touching the curb, as he did so, for security. It was but a motion of his fingers and no one could see it, but it made him confident that he had learned his lesson.

And in this way the phrase is made to undermine these two men, to reveal all their coarseness, their monotony of mind, their pompous ineptitude.

An acquaintance with *The Claverings*, then, is worth making not only for its own sake; it is probably the readiest way for a reader to sensitize himself to the subtler aspects of Trollope's style, and above all to his characteristic modes of irony. Without this sensitivity, none of his novels can be read rightly, for even in his dealings with the characters he knew and loved best—indeed especially· with them— this irony is never far away. But its quality is so quiet, its onset so unostentatious, that it can easily be missed.

For these reasons, then, these two novels seem to deserve attention. But it must at once be added that many of the others are as good, and very possibly better. *Ralph the Heir*, for example, has some fine political scenes, and at least one character, Sir Thomas Underwood, profounder in conception than any in *The Way We Live Now*. *The Belton Estate* is comparable with *The Claverings* in its compression, and has a parallel theme, the hesitations of a young woman between two lovers, developed with all that power of creating a dramatic scene which has been illustrated above in the encounter between the Archdeacon and Miss Crawley. Others of the lesser-known novels which certainly deserve to be much better known are *Orley Farm*, *Sir Harry Hotspur of Humblethwaite*, *Is He Popenjoy?*, *Dr. Wortle's School* and *Ayala's Angel*. The list could easily be made much longer, but the reader who wishes to explore these novels further has no lack of guides. If he is interested in the gloomier and less 'usual' aspects in them, he cannot do better than follow Mr. Cockshut; if, on the other hand, he prefers a more orthodox and central view, he should consult the *Commentary* of Mr. Michael Sadleir, to whom this generation owes much for defending and explaining a writer who seemed on the very point of slipping into oblivion.

But whatever he may choose to read, he should guard against two misconceptions which can prevent him from giving both himself and Trollope a fair chance. He should not, under the impression of length and weight of circumstance, mistake what is before him for mere photography, and so miss the real, though unostentatious imagination which has moulded it; nor should he let the apparent uniformity and directness of the style lull him into a hypnotic automatism, insensitive to those subtler turns of phrase which are so characteristic an expression of Trollope's 'moral consciousness', of his kindly but ironic perception of the gap between what we are, and what we ought to be, wish to be, or believe ourselves to be.

ANTHONY TROLLOPE

Select Bibliography

BIBLIOGRAPHIES

IRWIN, MARY L. *Anthony Trollope: A Bibliography*. New York: Wilson, 1926.
Contains useful references to early reviews, articles in periodicals, etc.

SADLEIR, MICHAEL. *Trollope: A Bibliography*. London: Constable, 1928.
Based on the compiler's renowned collection now in the Parrish Collection in the Princeton University Library. A pamphlet, *Addenda and Corrigenda to Trollope: A Bibliography*, was published in 1934, and there is additional material in Sadleir's *XIX Century Fiction* (Berkeley: University of California Press, 1951). The final authority on the works of Trollope themselves, with a fascinating section on the extent of their popularity, as measured by the book market.

GEROULD, W. G., AND GEROULD, J. T. *A Guide to Trollope*. Princeton: Princeton University Press, 1948.
Contains bibliographical tables, and a dictionary of characters, places, and events in the novels.

COLLECTED EDITION

There is no complete edition of Trollope's works, and it now seems unlikely that there ever will be, for the Oxford University Press has been forced to discontinue the Oxford Illustrated Trollope (1948–1954) at a point when it included only nine titles (in fifteen volumes). Many of the novels, however, with the *Autobiography*, are published in the World's Classics series by the same publishers, and for most purposes this can be regarded as the standard, if not complete, edition.

The Barsetshire Novels. Edited by Michael Sadleir. Shakespeare Head edition. 14 vols. Oxford: Blackwell, 1929.

SELECTIONS

The Trollope Reader. Edited by E. C. Dunne and M. E. Dodd. New York: Oxford University Press, 1947.
Gives few of his dramatic scenes, but exemplifies very well his range of observation.

The Parson's Daughter and Other Stories. Edited by J. Hampden. London: The Folio Society, 1949.
Includes *Katchen's Caprices*, not reprinted since its first appearance in *Harper's Weekly*, 1866–1867, and four other stories.

The Bedside Barsetshire. Edited by L. O. Tingay. London: Faber and Faber, 1949.
Has its uses, but proves very clearly that Trollope needs space and time to develop his effects.

Mary Gresley and Other Stories. Edited by J. Hampden. London: The Folio Society, 1951.
Includes five stories.

LETTERS

Letters. Edited by Bradford A. Booth. New York: Oxford University Press, 1951.

SEPARATE WORKS

Dates of first London editions are given, and modern editions and current paperbacks are also recorded here.

The Macdermots of Ballycloran. 3 vols. 1847. *Novel.*

The Kellys and the O'Kellys: A Tale of Irish Life. 3 vols. 1848. *Novel.*
The World's Classics.

La Vendée: An Historical Romance. 3 vols. 1850. *Historical Novel.*

The Warden, 1855. *Barsetshire Novel.*
Everyman's Library; The World's Classics; Nelson Classics; Oxford Illustrated Edition; Dolphin Paperback.

Barchester Towers. 3 vols. 1857. *Barsetshire Novel.*
Nelson Classics; The World's Classics; Oxford Illustrated Edition, 2 vols.; edited by Bradford Booth (Rinehart Edition, 1949); introduced by Michael Sadleir (Everyman Paperback, 1962).

The Three Clerks. 3 vols. 1858. *Novel.*
The World's Classics.

Doctor Thorne. 3 vols. 1858. *Barsetshire Novel.*
Everyman's Library; The World's Classics; Nelson Classics; edited by Elizabeth Bowen (Riverside Edition, 1960).

The Bertrams. 3 vols. 1859. *Novel.*

The West Indies and the Spanish Main, 1859. *Travel.*

Castle Richmond. 3 vols. 1860. *Novel.*

Tales of All Countries, 1861. *Stories.*
The World's Classics.

Framley Parsonage. 3 vols. 1861. *Barsetshire Novel.*
Everyman's Library; Nelson Classics; The World's Classics.

Orley Farm. 2 vols. 1862. *Novel.*
The World's Classics.

North America. 2 vols. 1862. *Travel.*
Edited by D. Smalley and Bradford A. Booth (New York: Knopf, 1951).

Tales of All Countries: Second Series, 1863. *Stories.*
The World's Classics.

Rachel Ray. 2 vols. 1863. *Novel.*
The World's Classics; New York: Knopf, 1952.

The Small House at Allington. 2 vols. 1864. *Barsetshire Novel.*
Everyman's Library; The World's Classics; Nelson Classics.

Can You Forgive Her?. 2 vols. 1865. *Novel.*
The World's Classics; Oxford Illustrated Edition, 2 vols.

Miss Mackenzie. 2 vols. 1865. *Novel.*
The World's Classics.

Hunting Sketches, 1865. *Sketches.*
Edited by J. Boyd (New York: At the Sign of the Gosden Head, 1933); and Lionel Edwards (New York: Day, 1953).

The Belton Estate. 3 vols. 1866. *Novel.*
The World's Classics.

Travelling Sketches, 1866. *Sketches.*

Clergymen of the Church of England, 1866. *Essays.*

Nina Balatka: The Story of a Maiden of Prague. 2 vols. 1867. *Novel.*
The World's Classics (with *Linda Tressel*).

The Last Chronicle of Barset. 2 vols. 1867. *Barsetshire Novel.*
Everyman's Library; Nelson Classics; The World's Classics; Norton Paperback.

The Claverings. 2 vols. 1867. *Novel.*
  The World's Classics.

Lotta Schmidt: And Other Stories, 1867. *Stories.*

Linda Tressel. 2 vols. 1868. *Novel.*
  The World's Classics (with *Nina Balatka*).

Phineas Finn the Irish Member. 2 vols. 1869. *Political Novel.*
  Everyman's Library; The World's Classics; Oxford Illustrated Edition.

He Knew He Was Right. 2 vols. 1869. *Novel.*
  The World's Classics.

Did He Steal It?, 1869. *Drama.*
  An adaptation by Trollope of the *Last Chronicle of Barset.* Edited by
  R. H. Taylor (Princeton: Princeton University Library, 1952).

The Vicar of Bullhampton. 2 vols. 1870. *Novel.*
  The World's Classics.

An Editor's Tales, 1870. *Stories.*

The Struggles of Brown, Jones and Robinson: By One of the Firm, 1870.
  Novel.
  A pirated edition had appeared in the U.S.A. in 1862.

The Commentaries of Caesar, 1870. *Translation.*

Sir Harry Hotspur of Humblethwaite, 1871. *Novel.*
  The World's Classics.

Ralph the Heir. 3 vols. 1871. *Novel.*
  The World's Classics.

The Golden Lion of Granpère, 1872. *Novel.*
  Everyman's Library; The World's Classics.

The Eustace Diamonds. 3 vols. 1873. *Political Novel.*
  The World's Classics; Oxford Illustrated Edition.

Australia and New Zealand. 2 vols. 1873. *Travel.*

Lady Anna. 2 vols. 1874. *Novel.*
  The World's Classics.

Phineas Redux. 2 vols. 1874. *Political Novel.*
  The World's Classics; Oxford Illustrated Edition.

Harry Heathcote of Gangoil: A Tale of Australian Bush Life, 1874. *Novel.*

The Way We Live Now. 2 vols. 1875. *Novel.*
  The World's Classics; New York: Knopf, 1950.

The Prime Minister. 4 vols. 1876. *Political Novel.*
  The World's Classics; Oxford Illustrated Edition.

The American Senator. 3 vols. 1877. *Novel.*
   The World's Classics.

Christmas at Thompson Hall. New York, 1877. *Story.*

South Africa. 2 vols. 1878. *Travel.*

Is He Popenjoy?. 3 vols. 1878. *Novel.*
   The World's Classics.

The Lady of Launay. New York, 1878. *Story.*

How the "Mastiffs" Went to Iceland, 1878. *Travel.*

An Eye for an Eye. 2 vols. 1879. *Novel.*

Thackeray. English Men of Letters. 1879. *Criticism.*

John Caldigate. 3 vols. 1879. *Novel.*

Cousin Henry. 2 vols. 1879. *Novel.*
   The World's Classics.

The Duke's Children. 3 vols. 1880. *Political Novel.*
   The World's Classics; Oxford Illustrated Edition.

The Life of Cicero. 2 vols. 1880. *Biography.*

Dr. Wortle's School. 2 vols. 1881. *Novel.*
   The World's Classics.

Ayala's Angel. 3 vols. 1881. *Novel.*
   The World's Classics.

Why Frau Frohmann Raised Her Prices and Other Stories, 1882. *Stories.*

Lord Palmerston. English Political Leaders. 1882. *Biography.*

The Fixed Period. 2 vols. 1882. *Novel.*

Marion Fay. 3 vols. 1882. *Novel.*

Kept in the Dark. 2 vols. 1882. *Novel.*

Mr. Scarborough's Family. 3 vols. 1883. *Novel.*
   The World's Classics.

The Landleaguers. 3 vols. 1883. *Novel.*

An Autobiography, 1883.
   The World's Classics; Oxford Illustrated Edition.

An Old Man's Love. 2 vols. 1883. *Novel.*
   The World's Classics.

The Noble Jilt: A Comedy. Edited by Michael Sadleir. London: Constable, 1923. *Drama.*
   Written in 1850, but never acted; used as the main plot of *Can You Forgive Her?* and mentioned in *The Eustace Diamond.*

London Tradesmen. Edited by Michael Sadleir. New York: Scribner's, 1928. *Sketches*.

From the *Pall Mall Gazette*, 1880.

Four Lectures. Edited by M. L. Parrish. London: Constable, 1938.

The Tireless Traveller. Edited by Bradford A. Booth. Berkeley: University of California Press, 1941.

Letters contributed to the *Liverpool Mercury*, 1875.

The Two Heroines of Plumplington. Edited by J. Hampden. New York: Oxford University Press, 1954. *Story*.

BIOGRAPHICAL AND CRITICAL STUDIES

MONTÉGUT, ÉMILE. *Écrivains Modernes de l'Angleterre*. IIIᵉ Série. Paris: Hachette, 1892.

Contains two reviews which first appeared in *Revue des Deux Mondes*, 1855 and 1858. The first of these reviews contains a long study of *The Warden*, the second deals fully with *Barchester Towers* and *Dr. Thorne*. They illustrate very clearly the general superiority of the French critical approach to fiction over that of the English reviewers of the same period. It was this superiority in skill and seriousness which enabled Montégut to perceive in Trollope, not simply a naïve realist, but a writer who imposed upon his report of life a pattern of his own, with a style of his own.

JAMES, HENRY. *Partial Portraits*. London: Macmillan, 1888.

The most perceptive of the early estimates of Trollope's quality.

HARRISON, FREDERIC. *Studies in Early Victorian Literature*. New York: Arnold, 1895.

A short essay, but of special interest because it gives a firsthand impression of Trollope himself, and of the surprise felt by the writer that such fine qualities should have happened to lodge in so bluff and noisy a man.

SAINTSBURY, GEORGE. "Trollope Revisited," *Essays and Studies*, Vol. VI (1920).

Copiously but indecisively corrects the same author's shallow and contemptuous essay in *Corrected Impressions*, 1895.

STEPHEN, LESLIE. *Studies of a Biographer*. Vol. IV. New York: Putnam's, 1902.

The essay on Trollope is short and pleasantly nostalgic; it treats him as a pleasing record of a peaceful but bygone age, and is the first expression of this mode of appreciating him.

STREET, G. S. *A Book of Essays*. Westminster: Constable, 1902.
A short essay on Trollope claims for him a higher place than was usual at the time, and discusses his "realism" with some penetration.

ESCOTT, T. H. S. *Anthony Trollope: His Work, Associates and Literary Originals*. New York: Lane, 1913.
The first full-length biography. Many details were filled in by a writer who knew Trollope personally.

NICHOLS, SPENCER VAN B. *The Significance of Anthony Trollope*. New York: McMurtrie, 1925.
Only 490 copies of this booklet were printed. Some of its literary judgements are too enthusiastic, but it contains one of the first attempts to draw a map of Barsetshire, and to classify the novels.

SADLEIR, MICHAEL. *Trollope: A Commentary*. Boston: Houghton Mifflin, 1927; revised edition, New York: Farrar, Straus, 1947.

WALPOLE, HUGH. *Anthony Trollope*. English Men of Letters. New York: Macmillan, 1929.

MACCARTHY, DESMOND. *Portraits*. New York: Putnam, 1931.

KOETS, C. C. *Female Characters in the Works of Trollope*. Amsterdam: van Tilburg, 1933.

STEBBINS, L. P., AND STEBBINS, R. P. *The Trollopes: The Chronicle of a Writing Family*. New York: Columbia University Press, 1945.
Contains much biographical information about Trollope's mother and his eldest brother Thomas Adolphus, and one of the first attempts to emphasize the gloomier and less orthodox strains in Trollope himself.

BOWEN, ELIZABETH. *Anthony Trollope: A New Judgement*. New York: Oxford University Press, 1946.

BROWN, BEATRICE C. *Anthony Trollope*. Denver: Swallow, 1950.
A sympathetic attempt to define the "theme" common to the novels, and some illuminating suggestions about the effect of civil service experience upon Trollope's approach to life and people.

COCKSHUT, A. O. J. *Anthony Trollope: A Critical Study*. London: Collins, 1955.

HELLING, R. *A Century of Trollope Criticism*. Helsingfors: Societas Scientiarum Fennica, 1956.
A detailed survey of the ups and downs of Trollope's reputation from his own day to the present, with a good selection of quotations from the original reviews, and a good bibliography of Trollope criticism.

BOOTH, BRADFORD A. *Anthony Trollope: Aspects of His Life and Work*. London: Hulton, 1959.

This very learned study is specially interesting on the social background, and the vagaries of Trollope's fame.

BOOTH, BRADFORD A. (ed.). *The Trollopian*. Los Angeles, 1945–1949.

A quarterly, continued after 1949 as *Nineteenth-Century Fiction*.

THE EARLY
NINETEENTH-CENTURY NOVEL

Select Bibliography

BAGEHOT, WALTER. *Literary Studies*. London: Longmans, 1879.
Everyman's Library, 2 vols.
Contains "Sterne and Thackeray," 1864, and "Charles Dickens," 1858—the latter probably the earliest of many comparisons between Dickens and Thackeray.

SAINTSBURY, GEORGE. *Corrected Impressions*. New York: Dodd, Mead, 1895.

ELTON, OLIVER. *Dickens and Thackeray*. London: Arnold, 1924.

SPEARE, M. E. *The Political Novel: Its Development in England and America*. New York: Oxford University Press, 1924.
The author is prevented from doing justice to Trollope by his admiration of Disraeli, whom Trollope disliked both as a politician and as a novelist.

BAKER, ERNEST A. *The History of the English Novel*. 10 vols. London: Witherby, 1924–1939.

QUILLER-COUCH, SIR ARTHUR. *Charles Dickens and other Victorians*. Cambridge: University Press, 1925.

CECIL, LORD DAVID. *Early Victorian Novelists*. New York: Bobbs-Merrill, 1935.
Valuable comparisons.

Nineteenth-Century Fiction, 1945—in progress.
A scholarly periodical. From 1945–1949 the title was *The Trollopian*.

LEAVIS, F. R. *The Great Tradition*. London: Chatto and Windus, 1948.
A controversial view of the Victorian novel.

TILLOTSON, KATHLEEN. *Novelists of the Eighteen-Forties*. Oxford: Clarendon Press, 1954.

PRAZ, MARIO. *The Hero in Eclipse in Victorian Fiction*. New York: Oxford University Press, 1956.

THOMSON, PATRICIA. *The Victorian Heroine: A Changing Ideal, 1847–1873*. New York: Oxford University Press, 1956.

STEVENSON, LIONEL. *The English Novel: A Panorama*. Boston: Houghton Mifflin Co., 1960.
Compact and modern survey.

STEVENSON, LIONEL. *Victorian Fiction: A Guide to Research*. Cambridge: Harvard University Press, 1964.

NOTE: Further studies and reference works are listed in: *The Cambridge Bibliography of English Literature*, 4 vols. (1941) and *Supplement* (1957); the Annual Bibliographies published in *PMLA* by the Modern Language Association of America; *The Year's Work in English Studies*, a survey of important critical books and articles, published annually for the English Association by Oxford University Press; the *Annual Bibliography of English Language and Literature*, an extensive listing of critical books and articles, published for the Modern Humanities Research Association by Cambridge University Press; William D. Templeman (ed.), *Bibliographies of Studies in Victorian Literature 1932–1944* (Urbana: University of Illinois Press, 1945); Austin Wright (ed.), *Bibliographies of Studies in Victorian Literature 1945–1954* (Urbana: University of Illinois Press, 1956); the Victorian Bibliographies published annually in *Modern Philology*, 1956 and 1957, and in *Victorian Studies*, 1957—in progress; the Selected Lists of Recent Publications in the *Victorian Newsletter*; and I. F. Bell and D. Baird (eds.), *The English Novel 1578–1956: A Checklist of Twentieth-Century Criticisms* (Denver: Swallow, 1959).

DATE DUE
